Terry Pattinson [was born in ...]ham in 1942. After a [...], he embarked upon [...] nineteen. Terry is [... D]aily Mirror, a post h[e ...] won the 'Scoop of th[e ...] into NUM President, [Arthur Scargi]ll's financial wheeler-dealing during and after the 1984 Miners' Strike.

Married with three sons, Terry lives with his wife Christine in Staines, Middlesex.

CONTENTS

Foreword	1
Preface	3
Acknowledgements	5
Introduction	7
One: What Is Sexual Harassment?	11
Two: Do the Victims Deserve It?	23
Three: Power over Women	41
Four: Attitudes to Women	69
Five: Two Women in a Man's World	77
Six: Sex Pests and a Rogues' Gallery	94
Seven: The Case of Tim Preston	105
Eight: Those Who Are Trying to Help	115
Nine: The Work of Diana Lamplugh	135
Ten: Fighting Back	150
Conclusion	172
Where to Get Help and Other Reading	174

FOREWORD

She was, I'd guess, sixteen or seventeen years old and a stunner. She wore a tight, tiny black leather skirt which skimmed her curvaceous bottom. Her clinging, low-cut T-shirt revealed her generous upper storey and the fluffy wild hair and heavy make-up plainly spelled sex-symbol.

She stepped into a lift at the office, followed by me and a middle-aged man. When she saw the man, her hips moved seductively in his direction and she flicked her hair. It was a perfect come-on. The man seemed embarrassed and uncomfortable and fled as soon as the lift paused.

I said 'Good morning, nice day' to the girl. 'Going to work?' I asked. 'Yeah,' she responded, sulkily. She wasn't a bit interested in having a conversation with me. I tried to stop myself from being condemnatory, from joining the 'she asks for it' brigade, because I do not belong to the group which says that any female who deliberately dresses to entice men asks for the trouble inevitably in store.

But I do have to try to be honest about women's attitudes. We women operate, at almost every level, in a male-dominated society — at home or at work.

I often think about women rifling through their wardrobes in the morning looking for something attractive to wear to the office. Presumably, in their subconscious minds, if not their conscious ones, they are hoping for approval from bosses and male colleagues. Rarely do women titivate for other women. It's doubtful if men rifle through their wardrobes hoping a grey suit and a natty tie will encourage women to treat them decently and fairly.

The truth, I think, is that most women know they risk unwelcome attention, but they hope to get *attention*. The leather-skirted kid was at the learning stage. She'll realise, as she grows up, what risks she's taking, and she'll learn to be wary, as we all do, even us Golden Oldies still toiling for a living.

Women are perceived as slaves — consciously or subconsciously — to be used and abused by their masters. I believe, without any evidence, that it was ever thus, but that until comparatively recently women remained silent, nervously accepting their fate.

In my own small experience, I have noted the changes in society, how only twenty years or so ago when I first began to write an advice column, wives wrote to me describing how they had to *submit* to their bullying husbands. Now, only very rarely is that word spelled out. Submission is no longer acceptable to today's women, thank God.

Today's women are stronger and tougher — which may well be one of the reasons why so many of them are victims of abuse by angry and frustrated men.

In trying to understand why it happens, not for a second can it be excused, let alone condoned. Sexual abuse at any level, from the cheap jibes at fellow workers on the factory floor to hideous rapes, must somehow be prevented.

My friend Terry's book is a must for every woman at work — indeed I think for every woman, for you can be as threatened in a supermarket as in the office or on the factory floor.

It is required reading for every man who has been tempted to sexually abuse a woman. It will help to guide and counsel the victims of this particularly unpleasant and frequently very frightening experience.

I wish I knew that young girl's identity so I could send her a copy. With my love.

Marje Proops

PREFACE

I fail to see why only a woman should be qualified to write about sexual harassment. Admittedly, the major victims of harassment are women, but because men are most commonly the harassers surely we, too, should be allowed a view?

Time after time women have pointed out to me that only a woman should be writing this book. One woman recoiled in horror when I informed her of my project. 'It will be ghastly if a man does it, full of filth and horrible detail,' she said.

I pointed out that the subject of sexual harassment will cover every point of view, ranging from the humorous to the serious, the sublime to the ridiculous, the facts and the myths. I have drawn extensively on recent case histories which illustrate the extent of the problem, both in this country and abroad. It is a world talking-point and one which clearly will never go away. Should we all sweep it under the carpet and pretend it does not exist? Should women be made to suffer it just because the problem has been with us for generations? Should they lose their jobs because of it? Lose promotion prospects and accept demotion because of it? Fall ill because of it? Move house because of it? Be scared to travel because of it? Should women dress dowdily because they are too frightened to look pretty? Should they be 'put in their place' in a male environment because the job is traditionally masculine and macho?

As with most books this one reflects a personal challenge, the desire to understand the motives behind the actions of the harasser and a genuine desire to help to 'do something about it'. Experts and pundits abound, while victims appear to multiply and cases pile up at the tribunals.

The expression 'sexual harassment' is fairly new in this country, although it has been familiar in the United States for just over a decade. It has become 'one of the major trade union issues of our time' according to a trade union leader friend of mine. For women, it is not just a workplace issue but one of the major issues of their lives. According to one victim, a woman train driver, some women 'die a thousand deaths' every day they go to work. From the cradle to the grave women have to learn how to cope with it, learn from it, and seek redress as a result.

Twenty years ago many people laughed, some women included, if a girl complained that she had been 'groped'. A typical response coming mainly from men was, 'She must have asked for it'. In recent months and years, however, cases have come to light proving that it is by no means a laughing matter for the victims. Although it is stating the obvious, we all have to accept that women are the main victims of unwanted sexual attention. Harassment of men by women is so rare that it is difficult to unearth examples.

If men are harassed they certainly keep very quiet about it. Ask a man if he has ever been sexually harassed and you will probably get the response 'No such luck' or 'Chance would be a fine thing'. Ask women the same question and you will hear stories long enough to fill the British Museum. Indeed, if something unpleasant has *not* happened to them you can be sure that they know of instances involving their friends, workmates, neighbours or relatives.

This was never intended to be an ambitious, academic enterprise. I merely felt it needed to be written, sometime, by somebody who regularly wrestles with the ramifications of the problem.

Terry Pattinson

ACKNOWLEDGEMENTS

My thanks to the following individuals and organisations, who have assisted me in compiling this book. Their tolerance and efforts on my behalf will always be remembered with deep gratitude.

Alfred Marks Bureau; Lynne Bryan, Press Officer, National Union of Public Employees; Myra Benson, Press Officer, Society of Graphical and Allied Trades (SOGAT) and former Press Officer, National and Local Government Officers' Association (NALGO); Maureen O'Mara, National Women's Officer, NUPE; Brenda Dean, General Secretary, SOGAT; Marjorie Proops and Christine Garbutt, journalists with the *Daily Mirror*; Ken Cameron, General Secretary of the Fire Brigades' Union (FBU); Andrew Dismore, Legal Advisor of FBU and lawyer for Lynne Gunning; Isolda McNeill, Labour Correspondent, *Morning Star*; Jo Richardson, Labour MP for Barking and spokeswoman for women's rights; Carol Foster and Fiona Fox of the Equal Opportunities Commission (EOC); Barry Howarth, Northern Regional Officer, NALGO; Barry Reamsbottom, Press Officer, Civil and Public Services Association (CPSA); Michael Rubenstein, Chairman of the Industrial Law Society, Co-Editor of *Equal Opportunities Review* and Editor of Industrial Relations Law Reports; Diana Lamplugh; Pat Turner, National Equal Rights Officer, GMB; Alan Sapper, General Secretary, Association of Cinematograph Trades and Technicians (ACTT); Labour Research Department; Pat Jones, Press Officer, Union of Shop, Distributive and Allied Workers (USDAW);

Heather Wakefield, former Women's Rights Officer, National Council for Civil Liberties; Mike Smith, Press Officer, Trades Union Congress (TUC); Valerie Mainstone, Women Against Sexual Harassment (WASH); Margaret Prosser, National Officer, Transport and General Workers Union (TGWU); Judy Secker, former Press Officer, Union of Construction, Allied Trades and Technicians (UCATT); National Union of Teachers; National Union of Journalists.

Finally, I would never have written this book without numerous friends and colleagues who have offered their critical encouragement, praise and abuse.

I particularly thank my friend, freelance journalist Brian Beckett, who pushed me along at times of despair. His idea this was.

Most indispensable, however, is my most harassed friend, my wife Christine, who has endured my solitary months of imprisonment in my study.

INTRODUCTION

Four summers ago I covered the annual conference of the clerical union, the Civil and Public Services Association in Brighton, Sussex. The CPSA, as it is known, represents lower-paid clerical grades in the Civil Service. It has a predominantly female membership and an overwhelming female presence at conference time. The press desk, on this occasion, was staffed entirely by men. The CPSA, a traditionally turbulent union, was not long in living up to its image. During a debate, a woman delegate complained that a male delegate had dropped his trousers at a social function the previous evening.

She launched into a tirade of abuse against this gentleman, whose name and place of employment she knew, and complained that his behaviour had ruined a good evening for many people. He was not fit to hold union office, she said, and should never again represent his branch at conference. Kate Losinska, the union President, reprimanded him publicly without naming him and the conference resumed.

This news item received a small amount of space in some newspapers, including the *Daily Mirror*, which employs me as an industrial writer, and in normal circumstances should have disappeared into the annals of history. However, the *News of the World*, an organ of veracity published by Rupert Murdoch, decided this was a matter of national importance. The news editor sent a reporter into the conference hall to interview the victim and her friends.

Why this attempted interview was not carried out

during the coffee break or lunch hour we will never know. The intrepid reporter concerned was determined, for some reason known only to him, to carry out his duties while the conference was in session and a debate was in progress. With one exception, we warned him of the folly of his actions.

The exception was the man from *The Daily Telegraph*, who pointed out the whereabouts of the aggrieved female. Pandemonium ensued. Clive Bush, the then CPSA Press Officer, unceremoniously bundled the man from the hall. The minor fracas resulted in the press, as a whole, being rebuked from the chair for gutter-press behaviour. In other words, we were all tarred with the same brush. The one thousand delegates howled with rage, hostile glances were directed at us and fists were raised. One man was restrained by stewards from approaching the press table. It was certainly not the sex pest he was after. It was us. For a few moments it all looked very dodgy, on a par with the time I accidentally and innocently gatecrashed a Freemasons' lunch.

Mrs Losinska, however, knew the score. She skilfully restored order and prevented the stewards from throwing us out. She weighed in with a fraternal speech, pointing out that we were not all like that man from the *News of the World*.

Later that day I saw the man who had dropped his trousers. He had a glass of beer in his hand, his mates were laughing loudly and he appeared to be a hero in their eyes.

Even at this stage, the pest had placed the germ of an idea in my mind.

But all this was small beer compared to the day in January, 1989, when I met an anxious woman official from NALGO, the town hall union. She told me that Tim Preston, Medical Records Officer at North Lonsdale Hospital, Barrow-in-Furness, had been dismissed for sexually harassing female colleagues. Would the *Daily Mirror* be interested in the story?

South Cumbria's health authority gave every help short of assistance, but, after several lengthy calls to the authority's General Manager, Richard Priestley, it was confirmed that Preston was dismissed for 'mismanagement with sexual harassment as a secondary factor'.

The fact that the health authority had attempted a Watergate-style cover-up and Preston himself had gone into hiding made it all the more intriguing. His victims, however, refused to stay silent. Soon they were relating their experiences in a crowded room, with the collective therapy clearly good for their morale. They were prepared to relate all the details, however embarrassing, in the presence of senior union officials and a journalist from Fleet Street.

They even threatened strike action if Preston was reinstated, such was their contempt for him.

They were determined to ensure that what he had done would become public knowledge and that he would find it difficult, if not impossible, to secure a position of power over women in future.

The courage shown by these women, assisted by the dogged determination of their male union official, convinced me that this was the tip of the proverbial iceberg. Subsequent research proved my instincts correct.

These women gave me the final inspiration for this book. My apologies, in advance, for any offence caused by views, research, opinions and facts which follow.

Levity, where inserted, is used simply to illustrate how wide-ranging this subject can be and in no way means to detract from the seriousness with which it is viewed by so many.

ONE

WHAT IS SEXUAL HARASSMENT?

The 'problem' of sexual harassment was first identified in the United States a decade ago and it has finally become recognized as one of the major issues in the lives of women, whether at work, at leisure or even at home.

Women are most commonly the victims, as men are the predators.

Both sexes maintain that what is harassment to one person may not be seen as harassment to another. The only real test is how the victim reacts to the unwelcome attentions of another and what she, or he, can and should do about it.

The sexual harasser is not always seeking sex, although that is a prime motivation in most cases. Chief motivation is all to do with power, in the vast majority of cases the power over women. This power covers a multitude of sins, including the power to belittle, keep somebody 'in their place', degrade and humiliate them, block their promotion prospects and even the power to dismiss and demote.

Before examining definitions I have no hesitation in confessing to my own early adventures as a typical male harasser, actions of which I am not proud, but which I ought to record. Fortunately for me it only took the form of 'wolf-whistling' as a teenager and I welcome this opportunity to congratulate the tough young female who quickly cured me of the habit.

Apart from threatening to punch me in the mouth, a positive form of direct action, she shouted: 'Have you lost your dog, son?' My friends thought this was hilarious and my embarrassment, as well as lasting until today, was enough to terminate my behaviour. Some men, unfortunately, are not so easily deterred and develop this hobby almost as an art form into adult life. 'They like it, really' is the common theme.

'Mild' harassment, unless stopped, can and does degenerate into far more appalling behaviour, resulting in sickness and even mental ill-health on the part of some victims.

More recently, I was rebuked by the secretary of Mick McGahey, former Vice-President of the National Union of Mineworkers. In a telephone conversation I had the audacity to call her 'pet', which is a Tyneside term of affection like 'hinney', 'mate' or 'marrer'. She scolded: 'I am not your pet.'

Thus rebuked, I apologised and retired hurt, after explaining that 'pet' was a form of Geordie endearment. Some might say she went 'over the top' by reacting as she did, while others might say, with justification, that for the second time in my forty-seven years I thoroughly deserved the reprimand.

Barman Ian Fraser, suffered an even worse fate than being reprimanded by Mick McGahey's secretary. He was fired by bosses at his power station social club for calling men 'petal' and women 'pet'. Ian was dismissed following complaints from drinkers.

His employers carried out an opinion poll and said he was the reason why trade had slumped. He was criticised in sixty of the replies. However, on Wednesday, 8 February, 1989, the father of three won £4,750 compensation for being sacked. He said later: 'For years I greeted the fellas as petal and the women as pet. It's a friendly way of saying hello.'

Before I analyse far more serious cases in detail, it is worth looking at the guidelines given in *Sexual Harassment at Work* published by the Trades Union Congress in August 1983, guidelines which have become the benchmark for codes of practice in unions and workplaces everywhere.

The unions' ruling body declares that a broad definition would include repeated and unwanted verbal or sexual advances, sexually explicit derogatory statements or sexually discriminating remarks made by someone in the workplace. These would be offensive to the worker involved, particularly if they caused the worker to feel threatened, humiliated, patronised or harassed, and would interfere with the worker's job performance, undermine job security, or create a threatening or intimidating work environment.

The TUC's guidelines say sexual harassment can take many forms including 'leering, ridicule, embarrassing remarks or jokes and unwelcome comments; suggestive remarks or other verbal abuse; leering at a person's body; compromising invitations; demands for sexual favours and physical assault'.

Such unwelcome comments can include remarks about dress or appearance, deliberate abuse, the offensive use of pin-ups, pornographic pictures, repeated and/or unwanted physical contact.

The TUC booklet says: 'Sexual harassment is a form of victimisation about which increasing concern is being expressed in the workplace. It is, in fact, a new name for a problem which is certainly not new. However, as the concern expressed about sexual harassment is relatively recent, many trade unionists have not yet recognised it as a serious problem. Indeed, it is often difficult to differentiate between a general sexist attitude within the workplace, and sexual harassment. Many trade unionists still regard it as a "fuss about nothing", something that is an inevitable consequence of men and women working together, or harmless fun.

'Social attitudes fail to recognise the difference between social interaction at work, which involves social relationships MUTUALLY [their emphasis] entered into, and sexual harassment which is the IMPOSITION of unwelcome attention or action on one person often by a person in a superior position. The occurrence of sexual harassment is, in general, a product of the position of, and reflects the attitude towards, women in society and in the workplace.'

These last two sentences are almost prophetic when looking at some case histories which we will study later.

The booklet argues that in spite of the Equal Pay and Sex Discrimination Acts, some women continue to be confined to the low-paid, semi-skilled and low-status jobs in service and 'caring' areas, while men predominate in the higher-paid supervisory and skilled jobs. It continues: 'In addition, women's right to play a full role within the workplace is still not firmly rooted in society's attitudes, and too often women workers are seen in terms of their family caring roles, or as sexually attractive objects, and not as workers attempting to earn a living. The prevalence of this attitude towards women as "lower status, secondary workers" can foster a situation where a male worker will use his actual or potential power over a female worker to "keep her in her place". In addition to their low status in employment generally, women also remain at the lower levels within the trade unions.

'Therefore, although unions can take steps to prevent, and immediate steps to tackle, cases of sexual harassment, ultimately the problem will only be resolved if accompanied by positive steps to achieve equality for women in employment and within their trade unions, and by ensuring that women are not used and treated as secondary workers.' It also makes the point that what is perceived as sexual harassment by one person may not be seen as such by another. And it says that different kinds of workplaces can also produce different experiences of sexual harassment.

The booklet explains: 'For example, often when sexual harassment is talked about it is in the context of the office where there is a clear cut division of status between female secretarial staff and male management, reinforced by the unwritten rule that the women workers have to look and dress attractively. However, there are many other instances of sexual harassment. For instance, teachers and other workers dealing with young people can face sexual harassment from them. Additionally, sexual harassment can result from the isolation of women in male dominated industries, or it can be a product of male resentment about a woman doing a particular job. The harasser may be in the same status job as the woman involved or in a lower status job than the worker against whom the unwanted attention is directed.

'In the latter circumstance harassment can be used as a weapon to undermine the authority of women supervisors, managers and tutors. The common link is that the action is unwanted by the woman. Sexual harassment is frequently a display of power over the recipient or is designed to undermine, isolate and degrade that person as a worker.'

The guidelines concede that the victims are not always women, but point out that because of the structure of British industry, the recipients are in the majority of cases female workers. However, the advice stresses that proposed action to alleviate sexual harassment is also applicable to men.

Results of such experiences often mean that women leave their jobs rather than face the harassment. In some cases they may be dismissed or lose promotion prospects for failing to comply with the suggestions made; and unwanted attention frequently creates a stressful and hostile working environment, which leads to mental and physical illnesses such as cystitis, headaches, digestive problems, nausea, general physical disability, and lack of resistance to infection.

The booklet emphasises that sexual harassment also undermines any attempt to achieve equality for women workers within a workplace. It adds: 'It can undermine many of the rights of workers for which trade unions have fought hard over the years, including the right of a healthy and safe work environment, equal treatment for women workers and freedom from discrimination on the grounds of sex. It is a legitimate concern for trade unions that the workplace can become a threatening environment for women, and trade unions have a duty to make members aware of, and sensitive to, the nature and scope of the problems involved, and to take action to prevent sexual harassment occurring.'

The TUC guidelines give some idea of the difficulties facing unions attempting to deal with the problem. They advise that sexist attitudes within a workplace can camouflage the severe effects that, for example, sexual taunts may be having on a particular woman.

The booklet continues: 'In addition, there is often the reluctance of the women to report [harassment] because they are ashamed and blame themselves as causing the action because they believe they will not be taken seriously. The more the question of sexual harassment is discussed in the open by trade unionists, both male and female, the easier it will become to eliminate it from the workplace.'

I was particularly interested in the penultimate sentence, because a young woman colleague of mine had an unpleasant encounter at work with an elderly male messenger. When I walked into the office the girl was on her own, white-faced and obviously upset. She told me that, for no apparent reason, the man had reached over the desk and touched her breasts. He had then left the office without saying a word. At first I was flabbergasted, because the man in question was known to me as a quiet, shy, retiring gentleman who kept himself to himself. My reaction was unfraternal. I wanted to punch him on the nose. The girl persuaded me not do anything rash on the grounds that she did not want to 'cause a fuss'. I pointed out that any 'fuss' had been started by him and not by her. She said: 'It would only get the union involved,' and lead to an internal disciplinary hearing at which she would have to give evidence. She doubted whether the print union concerned would believe her and thought that the management would be too scared to discipline him for fear of a strike.

I hasten to add that this incident took place before the introduction of Margaret Thatcher's trade union legislation and before the arrival of Robert Maxwell at the *Daily Mirror*. The local print union 'mafia' does not have the power to protect such a man today, and the workforce would not strike in support of such a man if he were disciplined.

The girl begged me to stay silent, but promised to let me know if he touched her or bothered her again. He did not and has since left on redundancy. Her case would have been covered perfectly by the TUC's 'sample clause' into the problem, given the will of employers and unions to implement it. A union branch official, preferably a woman, could have given her help and guidance, leading to a possible disciplinary hearing and the transfer of the harasser to another department.

About the same time as this incident, I heard about the case of a male office worker, described by his workmates as a 'wimp', who had complained to his NALGO union representative that he was being harassed by women workers at his office in Gateshead, Tyne and Wear. The women, apart from teasing him over his alleged lack of sexual prowess, had put pin-ups of themselves on the wall next to his desk. Some of the women had left compromising invitations. The photographs displayed the women in underwear and saucy night attire.

Eventually the man faced a nervous breakdown and, after discussions with an astounded management, he was transferred to the safety of another section where he was last reported working happily without harassment from anybody. Said a NALGO official: 'The poor fellow got no sympathy from any of the men in the building. Many said that they wished it had happened to them. Everybody is different, and it was surely no fault of his that he felt under pressure. He was cracking up under the strain.'

Whether represented by a union or not, some victims have been known to take direct action. A remarkable example of this was reported by my *Daily Mirror* colleague Peter Kane, when he covered the court case of secretary Dawn Blighton, who came close to exterminating office sex pest Anthony Luciznksas by lacing his lunchtime milk with Tippex. Dawn popped a few drops of the fluid into his 'pinta' after he called her the 'office tart'. What Dawn did not realise is that just a teaspoonful of Tippex can be lethal. Luciznksas was rushed to hospital with burns to his throat and lungs, and recovered. Dawn was sacked on the spot from her job with City stockbrokers Phillips and Drew.

At the Old Bailey she was charged with administering poison to Mr Luciznksas. The court heard that Dawn handed out the Tippex treatment after twice overhearing him say that she was 'sleeping around'.

She was let off with a conditional discharge after the judge was told she did not really mean to harm her colleague. Judge Nina Lowry told her: 'What you did was dangerous and stupid. I accept that you had some grievance, but the way you went about it was wrong. What you need to do is grow up and have more sense.' Dawn later told Peter Kane: 'I don't even have a boyfriend and this suggestion that I sleep around was very upsetting. I complained to the manager but he just shrugged his shoulders and did nothing about it. I had to put up with the bantering for three days and in the end my patience just snapped.

'I thought putting Tippex in his milk was just like putting salt in a drink instead of sugar. It was done as a prank.'

Dawn's experience was typical of so many suffered by women throughout industry, particularly young, attractive office workers. In this case the man used lies to undermine the young woman's reputation and confidence, and she had a boss typical of so many men. He just did not want to know, shrugged the problem off, and hoped it would go away. The result could have been the death of the harasser, when an office code of conduct, agreed by management and workforce, could have been enforced, have come to Dawn's assistance and the problem have been avoided.

Over on Merseyside, Liverpool City council employee Vince Birkhead was the centre of another storm, fully reported by the *Daily Mail* on 10 November, 1988.

The case almost blew up into a trade union war. The newspaper reported that the forty-one-year-old 'peace and pint-loving' bachelor was at the centre of a sexual harassment row which threatened misery for council house tenants in the city. It was a classic case of what is a union to do when the alleged harasser and victims are in the same union? Mr Birkhead was backed '110 per cent' by his union, the National Union of Public Employees. His branch secretary Billy Mills seemed in no doubt that Mr Birkhead had been wronged, describing him as the 'victim of women's lib turned hellish'.

But the National and Local Government Officers' Association, at the forefront of the sexual harassment debate, was firmly behind its 300 housing department members striking in sympathy with four women suspended for refusing to work with him. The suspended women refused to work with him at the local Dingle housing office because they had heard of his 'leering, ogling, history'. Because of this extraordinary dispute, 700 houses were said to be standing vacant and being vandalised. Mr Mills of NUPE insisted: 'Vince Birkhead stays where he is. We are quite satisfied that he is a normal male.' He added: 'It seems that a cat can look at the Queen but in some quarters a man cannot look at a woman. There are women's rights and equality, but there are men's rights too. This row is about sexual harassment and it is Vince who is being harassed. The only solution is for the entire male workforce to wear blinkers.'

The employer's solution? Mr Birkhead was transferred to a men-only office where, presumably, he is behaving himself.

The *Daily Mirror*'s Anne Robinson had her own

thoughts to offer in her column: 'When I started work 20-odd years ago there was no Sex Discrimination Act, no maternity leave and no detailed complaints procedure should the Editor choose to put his hand up your skirt. There was, however, another firm rule about skirts. This one roughly stated that, the shorter your mini, the greater the chances of the randy old so-and-so in charge ordering your name to be printed in large type next to the story you had written. Whether this worked out in practice I never really found out. Because, after eight weeks, I was fired. Not for incompetence, but for the more serious crime of marrying another member of the staff. I was out on my ear, jobless, penniless and without so much as a call from a union official.

'I was reminded of all this when Liverpool City housing offices came to a standstill over Mr Vince Birkhead. Mr Birkhead, according to female NALGO members, undressed women with his eyes. And 300 of them walked out in protest. Mr Birkhead, on the other hand, claims he is being persecuted by militant feminists. Liverpool City Council, meanwhile, say they can find no evidence against Mr Birkhead but, in order to pacify NALGO members, they have given him compassionate leave. Mr Birkhead, therefore, is at home with only his mum to look at, until he can be found a job in an all-male office. So, is this progress?

'Should we cheer that, after two decades, along with fair and proper job safeguards for women who marry and those who become pregnant, we no longer have to suffer the office lech? I don't believe so. True progress would surely mean the office lech no longer existed. But he does. You'd be hard put to find an office without one. And, invariably, complaints against him bring forth the countercharge of loony women with more imagination than sense. What 20-odd years have taught me is that ridicule and humour, rather than official action, is the fastest route to curing this problem. And how much more effective if the female members of NALGO at the Dingle housing office, who were so apparently offended by Mr Birkhead's behaviour, had simply cornered him one morning and removed his trousers for the rest of the day.'

The view of Mr Birkhead is worth recording in full, because it shows clearly how some men simply cannot see that what they are doing can in any way be offensive to women. He said: 'None of the four women can accuse me of ogling them. How could I? As I arrived, they left. One of them had told the others of the rumours and that was it. Beware idle gossip. It can ruin a man. I will be vindicated, believe me. But will that convince Joe Public now that I have been branded as some sort of monstrous sex maniac? The claim is that I undress women with my eyes. It is ridiculous. If all women who work alongside me took their attitude Britain would grind to a halt.

'Is there one man worthy of the name who hasn't looked at and admired a woman? But when militant feminists are on the loose we are expected to become robots.'

Mr Birkhead said that in twenty-one years with Liverpool City Council he could think of no instances which could remotely be construed as familiarity. He remembered placing his arm briefly around the waist of a woman colleague in a gesture of friendship.

Let us give the hapless Mr Birkhead the benefit of the doubt, but it is a fact that some men do undress women with their eyes. I have seen it happen and I have seen the way women look away in fear and embarrassment. Women feel threatened by this behaviour and it cannot do much for their confidence in the workplace. It is something men do not have to endure.

Women, on the other hand, can do a lot to help themselves, particularly in the office environment where they are expected by many male bosses to look attractive.

One young woman, currently working 'casual' shifts in the *Mirror* headquarters, has a penchant for micro-mini skirts which display her shapely legs. The eyes of the men follow her wherever she goes and you don't need special mental powers to work out what is going on in some of the minds of the beholders. When she catches their stares she makes pathetic attempts to tug down the skirt, which is little more than a belt around her waist. This futile attempt at hiding her embarrassment only serves to focus the attention on what she is trying to cover up. Of course, she is welcome to dress how she likes without the fear of harassment and the men should learn to keep their eyes to themselves. But is it expecting too much to ask people of both sexes to dress with common sense at work?

When I am trying to concentrate on the unemployment figures and the Ford pay strike should I really have to see bare female thighs, bra-less tight sweaters, frilly knickers, stocking tops and suspenders? If you wave a red rag at a bull don't be too surprised if it charges. I am a class-one soccer referee and I firmly believe that harassment can be prevented in cases of 'provocative' dress if both sides play the game fairly. A tiny minority of women, in my view, don't do a lot to help themselves and the attention they clearly crave can result in dangerous situations they have not bargained for.

This, as you will see, is my only criticism of some members of the female sex. I realise that such an opinion may cause offence, but it is, nonetheless, one in which I firmly believe. I have also been surprised at the number of women, like the *Daily Mirror*'s Marje Proops, who agree with this view. Indeed, women's biggest critics as to how they dress would appear to be other women.

TWO

DO THE VICTIMS DESERVE IT?

'She was looking for it', 'She got what she deserved' and 'You can't blame the men for wanting her' are typical quotes from men when a woman, 'who has dressed provocatively', is attacked in any way.

Actress Jodie Foster starred in a film called *The Accused* in which a girl was gang-raped. The girl in the film dressed 'provocatively', danced erotically and teased men in a bar. They assaulted her more out of revenge rather than lust, according to reviewer Margaret Walters in *The Listener*. Frankly, I did not bother to view that particular film because I feel that certain modern pictures are becoming too voyeuristic. I appreciate, however, that many film-goers like this form of entertainment and that there is little point in burying one's head in the sand when it comes to important issues like the one depicted in *The Accused*.

Journalist Suzanne Moore, writing in the *New Statesman*, made an excellent point when reviewing *The Accused*. She wrote: 'What this shows, once and for all, is that rape has very little to do with sex and everything to do with power. Rape is not an isolated act. It exists on a continuum of sexual abuses and harassment that works to imprison women both physically and mentally.

'*The Accused* challenges the myth that a woman who is raped may be "asking for it" — a ridiculous fallacy in a society which still makes it extremely difficult for women to ask for anything, a society that doesn't hear when women do ask for what they want, a society in which male desires not only impose themselves on female desire, but depend on cancelling female desire out.

Asking for it? If only we could ...'

Nevertheless, we must question whether pictures like this ultimately do any good. Are would-be rapists likely to desist from their behaviour after seeing such films? Indeed, are certain categories of men 'turned on' by these movies? Peter Cook, the convicted Cambridge rapist, admitted that a *Kojak* television episode gave him the idea to rape while disguised as a woman. More recently, a teenage boy admitted sexually assaulting a young girl passer-by because he was sexually aroused by a 'girlie magazine'. Ultimately, I wonder whether the girlie-mag models and the Jodie Fosters of this world are doing their fellow females a favour?

The effects of freely available pornographic magazines, and the effects women's choice of dress has on men, were raised at the Old Bailey on 30 October, 1989. Outraged MPs demanded action against pornography after three rapists were jailed for a total of thirty-nine years. In this particular case the three men had apparently acted out a sex fantasy after luring two teenage convent schoolgirls to a flat and plying them with drink and cannabis. The girls' ordeal spotlighted what many women have always feared, that hard-core pornography can trigger serious sex crimes.

MPs called for new restrictions on the sale of pornographic material and demanded an investigation into links between pornography and sex offences. Dame Jill Knight, a Tory MP, said newsagents should curb sales of pornography, which she claimed had a proven link with many brutal sex crimes, while Joan Ruddock, Labour, said: 'The association of violence and sex in these magazines is clearly dangerous to women.'

The rapists, all from South London, were Gifford Titre, twenty-six, who already had a record for rape and robbery dating back to 1980, adventure playground worker Carl Davids, thirty, and building worker Brian Hope, twenty-seven. Titre and Davids were sentenced to fourteen years, while Hope was sentenced to eleven years. Judge Nina Lowry told them: 'It is difficult to calculate the emotional injury to the girls or to foresee the remaining effect. I have to consider members of the public, women and girls.'

During the month-long trial the court heard that the three men had been cruising around in a van and spotted the girls, chatted to them, and persuaded them to go to Hope's flat where they were introduced to drink, cannabis and shown 'blue movies'. James Curtis, prosecuting, said: 'It seems that some men get the feeling that if a girl is wearing a short skirt she is more ready to be friendly.' The girls had been 'bored with nothing to do' and did not spurn the men's initial attentions. Said Curtis: 'It was a little bit of mild excitement for the girls. The last thing they expected was a sexual adventure. They were just two ordinary, respectable girls. It was a cold and determined assault. The girls were somewhat inebriated. They were not in a position to think straight or to fight back, certainly not against three fit and healthy men.'

After two and a half hours the girls were ejected from the flat and told to go home. Hope offered them five pounds for their bus fare and told them: 'Just think of it as a good time'. The next day they telephoned the Samaritans and the police were called. A magazine was discovered in Hope's flat and in it was a fantasy story about girls being accosted in the street by men and taken to a flat for group sex. Said Curtis: 'That is terribly similar to the ordeal suffered by those girls.'

Commenting on the case Jill Knight told the *Daily Mail*: 'For a long time many of us have been telling the obvious truth that pornography distorts the balance of the mind. I am aware of the freedom argument over pornography but I am also aware that girls should be able to walk out without being raped. How many more of these incidents must we have?' Former Labour frontbencher Clare Short, a campaigner against Page-3 pin-ups, said: 'More should be done to investigate the link between sexual offences and pornography. This has been proved time and time again, and nothing has been done.' Dame Peggy Fenner, Tory MP for Medway, concluded: 'This is a particularly horrible case. I worry terribly about the climate of pornography in this country and there can be little doubt of a link between it and the increase in violent sexual offences. I believe it can have a very damaging effect on people of a less than stable mind. There have been a number of cases where hard-core pornography has been found in the homes of convicted sexual offenders and it is deeply worrying.'

Hilary Bonner, Showbusiness Editor of the *Daily Mirror*, has made the point that however a woman is dressed, and however she may behave, she does not deserve to be raped. Similarly, she could point out that a man carrying one million pounds in a suitcase at midnight in a Glasgow side street does not deserve to be mugged or sexually harassed. And I would agree. I would take time off, however, to ask the man with a million pounds why he was carrying it about in a suitcase in a Glasgow side street at midnight. I might say: 'Were you not tempting fate?' Police would probably ask the same question, as would the man's insurance company and bank manager. The same question, in my opinion, could legitimately be put to a woman dressing and behaving like Jodie Foster.

Nobody deserves to be sexually harassed and, judging from all the evidence, most people do not 'go looking for it'. Harassment finds them. Marjorie Proops, Fleet Street's most famous agony aunt, feels that women could do a lot to help themselves, and says so quite bluntly in the foreword to this book. Marje told me: 'A lot of women think I am not the friend of women and am not on their side, but believe me, I am.' Marje feels that women could dress 'sensibly' for work and I agree.

Marje was in the office canteen one morning when she noticed a young waitress in a black-and-white eye-catching, figure-hugging outfit. The girl's garb left little to the imagination — men's imagination, that is. 'The men could not take their eyes off her. She was the sole topic of conversation. She was the sexiest thing in the building,' said Marje.

Many women will declare that they should be free to dress how they like at work, but do not circumstances alter cases? I have seen schoolchildren and men dress outrageously at school and work and I have seen them suffer from the headmasters' and bosses' rebukes as a result. They were all forced to conform to the authorities' wishes in the end. Why shouldn't this form of discipline, which really ought to be self-discipline, be enforced at work?

In my thirty years of working in office environments all over Britain I have seen women dressing to 'follow fashion'. The very thought of attracting men, according to my sister, had never entered her head when she was a teenager. I again retain the right to remain sceptical.

An attractive secretary arrived one day at my office at the *Daily Express*, my former newspaper. She wore a Chinese-style dress split to the hip, had a large flower in her hair and she was adorned with huge gold earrings, gold bracelets and a low neckline. Fingers and toenails, peeping out of sandals, were painted bright red. She clearly wanted to be noticed, if not remembered. She said: 'Do you think I am overdressed for work? Some of the other girls have been getting at me.' I replied 'Yes', and she did not speak to me for a fortnight.

Valerie Mainstone, of the campaigning organisation Women Against Sexual Harassment (WASH), an organisation we will look at in the next chapter, dismisses myths that women 'ask for it' in the way they dress or behave or that sexual pressures are too much for some men to handle. She said: 'It is not the posters on the walls that attack women, it is the men. Women should be allowed to dress how they like without the risk of being groped or worse and they should certainly not have to cover themselves from head to foot in sacks. In any case, women are frequently sexually harassed without wearing the type of clothing which some men describe as sexy and provocative.'

Barclays Bank, not in any way in sympathy or collusion with this writer, started a rumpus when bosses warned women employees not to wear 'provocative' clothes at work in a bid to reinforce a 'sober image'. The ban on 'mini, mini-skirts' and stilleto heels was included in a two-page memo on dress for women and men in the 6,000-strong Barclaycard division. Men were told to wear suits and sports jackets, a shirt and tie, with tattoos worn by both sexes to be covered at all times.

The bank clerks' union, BIFU, was incensed. Said a spokesman: 'It's the suggestion that male managers can be provoked by the clothes female staff wear that so annoys us. We believe women are sensible enough to choose their own clothes in an office environment.' David Buxton, Director of Personnel for the bank's central retail services division, said the dress code had been prepared with 'common sense and propriety in mind'. He said denim jeans, corduroy trousers, training shoes and dungarees were unacceptable.

The Equal Opportunities Commission (EOC) said the use of the word 'provocative' was 'unfortunate' and that the bank was treading a 'very dangerous line'. The union claimed that, in negotiations, Barclays management dismissed the EOC's criticisms and went on to say that 'provocative clothes might be overly attractive and cause ogling'.

Most people will share the view of the EOC and agree with Valerie Mainstone's argument, as does this author. What Valerie refuses to consider, however, is the degree of risk involved in 'dressing how you like'. My colleague Mary Riddell says: 'A woman should be allowed to dress how she likes, where she likes, whenever she likes' and, on the face of it, it seems churlish to disagree with that basic, democratic freedom. But do parents allow their teenage daughters to dress how they like, whenever they like and wherever they like? The answer is no, because the parents exercise their instincts to protect their brood from predators — namely men. My point is best illustrated by the following case from America.

The young woman in question, Blondina Ortega, twenty-two, was not 'looking for it', nor did she deserve it. She exercised her democratic freedom to dress how she liked, wherever she liked and whenever she liked. A jury in Fort Lauderdale, America, freed the man accused of rape because they said his mini-skirted victim 'provoked him' by her dress. The extraordinary case was highlighted in the *Mail On Sunday* newspaper on 8 October, 1989 by journalist Mike McDonough. Blondina was described as an innocent convent-educated girl who was kidnapped, beaten and raped by twenty-six-year-old Steven Lord, a man with a history of arrests for sex crimes. After watching her attacker reprieved, she told of the court ruling that blackened her name. She said: 'The truth is I was kidnapped. I was beaten. I was almost murdered before being raped three times.

'My life has been ruined, not only by the brute who raped me but by a jury who decided I was to blame because of what I was wearing. That jury made me feel dirty for wearing fashionable clothes — a white lace miniskirt and a green tank top. Yet they are the sort of clothes girls everywhere dress in every day. Does that mean they deserve to be raped?'

McDonough reported that Blondina had watched the award-winning film *The Accused* with her friends, but did not believe that anything like that would happen to her. Blondina, said McDonough, lived comfortably on income from a trust set up by her wealthy South American father. He described her as 'well-groomed, decent, intelligent ... from a close-knit Catholic family'.

Blondina recalled what happened in November 1988, when, in the early hours of the morning, she was confronted by Lord in a car park near her apartment in a quiet suburb of Fort Lauderdale. 'I had been to the movies and I stopped at a fast food restaurant at 3 am to get a meal. I had taken two steps out of the car when he came up behind me and put a knife in my back. He said that if I didn't do it I would be killed. He forced me back in the car and started driving. During the next five hours he slashed my face, hit me over the head with a rock, leaving me drifting in and out of consciousness, and raped me.

'I remembered the advice that women should not fight a rape attacker so I just tried to block what was happening from my mind. When the car crashed early in the morning the impact brought me round. For the first time since he grabbed me the knife was not there. So I ran free, screaming.'

Blondina was terrified when she saw her attacker in court. But she was not there when the jury, half of it female, made its astounding ruling accusing her of 'advertising for sex' by her dress. She said: 'When I heard what they said about me I hid away for two days. I am a decent girl, trying to live a decent life and I believed until then that the decent people of the jury would protect me. It is so unjust. I would like to face every member of that jury and ask them why they did this to me. I have been physically raped by a monster and emotionally raped by the system. Before the rape I was a happy twenty-two-year-old with everything to look forward to. Now I am scared to go out alone, scared to drive my car. I worry that my case has given every pervert out there a licence to rape any woman who dresses in a manner they think is provocative.'

At the end of the case Lord was led away in handcuffs, laughing, to stand trial for other sex offences.

The court decision, of course, was ludicrous. In my opinion, Lord should have been sentenced to life, or at least thirty years in jail. Blondina was lucky to escape with her life.

Blondina's father called her 'intelligent'. I call her *naïve*. Had she been so cocooned in her convent that, at twenty-two, she did not know she was living in a lawless society, a society so brutal that little has changed from the days of the Wild West? Would Blondina have walked through a field of bulls waving a red flag? Had she been kept away from radios, TV sets and newspapers all her life?

I was picked up by police when I took a stroll through Beverly Hills, Los Angeles, one sunny afternoon and told I was lucky not to have been mugged, or worse. The police told me that people in America went around in cars and that only 'vagrants' were on foot. They warned me not to place myself at risk and I heeded their warning. I was disappointed, because I wanted to exercise my democratic freedom to walk where I liked, when I liked and, yes, dressed how I liked.

My only criticism of Blondina is that she placed herself at risk unnecessarily in a violent world. All of us, at the end of the day, must take some steps to protect our own safety bearing in mind the cruel society around us. We can do ourselves a favour, and keep our relatives' and friends' minds at rest, by doing so much to help ourselves. The hard-pressed police and worried parents would probably agree. Going out at 3 am wearing a mini-skirt, alone, will not endear you to the on-duty policeman.

I end the sermon here because I want to stress, and stress again, that men do not have to suffer the sexual pressures faced by women. Our careers do not depend on whether we arrive for work looking like a member of the supporting cast of *Suzy Wong* and our regrading does not hinge on whether we have refused to go to bed with the boss.

Further examples I include, from recent case histories, are typical of the many pouring through tribunals, the courts, and the pages of the national and local press. I mention them to show how widespread the 'problem' has become and how varied are the cases. I do not necessarily publish them to prove a point in any particular context.

*

The problem of pornography was raised by the Businesswomen's Travel Club, a travel watchdog organisation which complained about porn movies in hotels. Under a headline 'Banish Hotel Porn to Save Career Girls from Gropers', the *Today* newspaper said on 3 July, 1989: 'Sexy films shown in hotels are a nightmare for businesswomen, it was claimed yesterday. They encourage lonely men to harass female guests in the bars, seeing them as "easy game". Many are forced to flee their rooms and are now demanding that hotels "clean up or close up."' The paper's Andrew Young said: 'Women executives also complain that they are treated like prostitutes by doormen and given no extra security during visits. Women make up thirty per cent of the business travel trade and are mostly under forty and single, whereas their male counterparts tend to be over forty and married.' The Club's spokeswoman Trisha Cochrane declared: 'Businessmen have left their wives at home and see single women in the bar as easy game. Many women sit in their rooms, too scared to go for a drink because they will be harassed.

'Porn films on video, cable and satellite television give men ideas. Many hotels try and show them after the bar closes, but women still feel vulnerable.' She said doormen often ask women for evidence that they are staying in the hotels because they suspect they are prostitutes. Trisha added: 'That is ridiculous. They never ask men.'

Sex therapist Angela Martin commented: 'Porn films can lead men into thinking single women want attention', but she warned women can often misconstrue men's intentions. 'Many are lonely and just want a chat but women see it as a sexual advance.' Andrew Young said: 'Hotel chains hit back, claiming they respond to women's needs.' He quoted Janet Edwards of Crest Hotels: 'Our chain has never had any complaints. Films we show are the same in the cinema and screened after the bar closes.

There is a demand for them from customers. Our staff are trained to subtly intervene if they spot a woman getting into unwanted attentions.' A Holiday Inn official added: 'You can see much worse on Saturday night TV. Our films are not the sort that would incite any loutish behaviour.'

Trusthouse Forte stated that they refuse to show 'adult films' because 'We are a family business'.

Rape is an extreme example of sexual harassment and there is frequently only a gossamer thread of difference between harassment and a serious sexual assault. It is a fact that women are as much at risk in the home, where a husband's power can be every bit as threatening, if not more so, than the power of a stranger. There are many who believe, like myself, that rape within marriage, or between common-law partners, should be punished just as severely as rape by a stranger or someone outside the immediate family.

On Thursday, 14 March, 1991, the common-law principle, dating back to 1736, that husbands cannot be guilty of raping their wives, was rejected by the Court of Appeal. The decision by the five-judge court, headed by Lord Lane, the Lord Chief Justice, upheld the wife's right to refuse consent, and abolished the husband's remaining immunity in England and Wales. Their decision brought England and Wales into line with Scotland, where judges decided in 1989 that there was no longer any marital immunity to the law of rape. Lord Lane said that the idea that a wife, by marriage, consents in advance to her husband having sexual intercourse whatever her state of health, or however proper her objections, was no longer acceptable. He said: 'It can never have been other than a fiction, and fiction is a cruel basis for criminal law.' He said the time had come for the law to declare that 'a rapist remains a rapist subject to the criminal law, irrespective of his relationship with his victim'. He added: 'This is not the creation of a new offence. It is the removal of a common-law fiction which has become anachronistic and offensive and we consider that it is our duty having reached that conclusion to act upon it.'

In the test case before them the judges dismissed an appeal by a thirty-seven-year-old Leicester man jailed for three years for attempting to rape his estranged wife. He had pleaded guilty after the trial judge, Mr Justice Owen, ruled that by the circumstances of their separation, the wife had withdrawn her implied consent to sexual intercourse given before marriage. The five judges agreed that the case raised an issue of law of public importance and granted the husband leave to appeal to the House of Lords, which was not opposed by Mr John Milmo, QC, counsel for the Director of Public Prosecutions, Sir Allan Green, QC. This meant that a final decision depended on the views of the Law Lords, whose ruling was expected later in 1991.

ITV producer Dorothy Byrne, who wrote an excellent campaigning article in *The Listener* on 28 September, 1989, examined *World in Action's* survey of 1,000 married women in which ninety-six per cent of them argued that rape within marriage should be a crime. 'It's a natural assumption. Try to think of another act of violence which is not defined as criminal.

'The married man's exemption is usually attributed to Sir Matthew Hale, a 17th-century judge, who justified it in the following terms: "The husband cannot be guilty of rape committed by himself upon his lawful wife, for by their mutual matrimonial consent and contract the wife has given up herself in this kind unto her husband, which she cannot retract." Of course, there are other arguments. Chief among them is that rape by a husband is not nearly as serious as "real rape" by a stranger.

'This was the view taken by Sir Frederick Lawson, chairman of the Criminal Law Revision Committee which recommended, in 1984, that the law should stay as it is for married couples living together.

'Sir Frederick was asked why he felt being raped by a

husband was not as bad as rape by a stranger. He replied: "Using my common sense and knowledge of the world." In the survey, 1,000 married women, who presumably also had some common sense and knowledge of the world, were asked what they thought. Eighty-four per cent said rape by a husband and rape by a stranger were equally serious. It was made clear in the survey that women were not being asked about a wife being asked to have sex reluctantly — but about forced sex against a woman's will.'

Dorothy Byrne pointed out that in the days when husbands could not be charged with rape, they pleaded guilty to assault. In one instance, a man who raped his wife was given a 150-hour community service order for bruises he caused during the rape. She continued: 'One unfortunate woman recently appeared in an article headlined, "Kinky Sex Terror of Bound Blonde". A full description of her rape was given, as were her name and place of work. This was possible because her husband was charged not with rape but with false imprisonment and indecency. Byrne argued that many women had been terrified and degraded by their husband's sexual assaults over a period of years but they thought they just had to put up with this. Two-fifths of marital rape victims in the survey had told nobody about what had happened.

Paul Wilenius, Political Editor of *Today*, said that two million of Britain's thirteen million married women had been raped by their husbands 'according to unofficial estimates', while crime expert Kate Painter, of Manchester University, was quoted in the *Sun* on 5 February, 1991, as saying that five per cent of wives had sex with their menfolk after violence was threatened or carried out. She found that wives were seven times more likely to be raped by their husbands than by a stranger.

Prior to the historic change in the law, Barbara Cohen, a lawyer with the Haldane Society, a legal reform group, wrote to the Home Office saying that wives raped by their husbands should have legal protection from vicious cross-examination in court. She said: 'While the rape victim remains the central character in the court case, at the moment she is not legally represented and protected like the attacker. Without far-reaching changes in this area, recognition of rape in marriage will not work.'

Critics who had forecast that such cases could not easily be proven were shown to be wrong only a fortnight after the Appeal Court law change, when a husband was jailed for five years after raping his wife. The thirty-three-year-old lorry-driver from south-east London was sentenced at the Old Bailey for a drunken assault on his twenty-three-year-old estranged wife while armed with a kitchen knife. A jury of eight men and four women took four hours and thirteen minutes to find him guilty of rape at the end of the five-day trial. They also convicted him of indecent assault.

Judge Brian Capstick said: 'I appreciate that no two cases are the same and take into account that a rapist is a rapist irrespective of the relationship he has with his victim.' Jonathan Turner, for the Defence, said, in his closing speech to the jury, that the change in the law had opened up a legal minefield. 'It is difficult enough in an ordinary case of rape to decide the issue and put aside emotion. How much more difficult it is in a case where the parties are married to one another.' He said wives who wanted a quick divorce and improve their chances of getting custody of children might now falsely accuse their husbands.

The wife was in tears in the witness box when she described how she was forced to have intercourse and oral sex after allowing her husband to spend the night on a sofa in a separate room. They had been married for ten months, but the relationship had run into difficulties. The man, found guilty by a ten to two majority, blinked hard, turned pale, and looked close to fainting before going to the cells.

In an exclusive interview the young mother told the

Daily Mirror's Lorraine Butler: 'All the pain and torment I went through was worthwhile. I wanted to see justice done. I am absolutely overjoyed with the verdict. He will hate me, but it's all his own fault. The whole ordeal has been degrading and humiliating. I just hope this gives other women who have suffered what I have the courage to report their husbands for rape.' Lorraine said that the husband, who admitted to a ten-pints-a-night drink problem, raped his wife at her South London home only hours before she was due to see her solicitor about a legal separation. Her four-year-old son wept in terror during the attack. The couple had split up a fortnight earlier and the man claimed his wife had agreed to have sex 'one more time'.

Mr Turner, the husband's barrister, told the jury that apologies were due to millions of wives who had been raped by their husbands over the centuries.

How can anyone divorce sex discrimination from sexual harassment? Millions of women have discovered, to their cost, that being born female often works against them in a male-dominated society, particularly when jobs, promotion, and child-bearing are concerned. Sex discrimination, in my view, can justifiably be seen as a form of sexual harassment, and a case in Scotland, involving Mrs Jean Porcelli, bears this out. We will study her case fully later, but I believe the case of Liz Berrisford, twenty-one, is worth looking at in the context of this chapter. Did Liz really deserve this?

School matron Liz was sacked after she told her boss she was about to become an unmarried mother. Headmaster Alan Grigg at first congratulated her, but when she said she had no plans to marry, he consulted the school governors and they decided she had to leave. The *Daily Mirror*'s Rod Chaytor reported her case on 1 November, 1989. She told Chaytor: 'I would not have lost my job if I had been a man. No one would think of sacking a bloke who was an unmarried dad.' A furious

Liz, who had worked at the exclusive St Mary and St Anne girls school at Abbots Bromley, Staffordshire, for just over a year, claimed her dismissal was sex discrimination. After she became pregnant she and her boyfriend decided to split up.

She continued: 'I went to the headmaster's study and told him I was expecting a baby. He said, "Congratulations" and asked me when I would wed.

'When I told him I had no immediate wedding plans he seemed surprised. Later he told me I would be setting a bad example to the girl pupils and asked me to leave.' Headmaster Grigg said: 'I know this is 1989 but there are still some people who believe that unmarried motherhood is not right. We did not think it the right example to place before our girls at an impressionable age.'

An official of the Department of Employment told Chaytor: 'She might have a claim for sex discrimination if she could prove that a man in a comparable position would not have been sacked.'

The headmaster will, I have no doubt, be praised by some for having the courage to set and maintain standards in his own school. But one day, perhaps, it will not be seen as a crime or a disgrace to be an unwed mother. And better still, it might cease being grounds for dismissal.

On 14 August, 1989, *The Daily Telegraph* ran the following story: 'Many secretaries suffer from office stress, according to a new survey. They have to put up with constant interruptions, over-demanding bosses, uncomfortable offices, equipment breakdowns and smokers, it found. One in four said they were subjected to harassment by the office wolf. The survey quizzed 312 secretaries on stress at work. A consumer psychologist, Sue Keane, who carried out the survey for Kall-Kwick Printing, said: "No secretary can fulfill her potential if she is working in stressful conditions."' And she told the *Daily Mirror*: 'How can a sexually harassed secretary be expected to work efficiently?'

One man in the perfect position to answer that is sex pest boss Owen Brown, just the right example of the type of man I will be discussing at great length in this book. Brown, thirty, and married with two children, 'made life hell' for his secretary Carolyn Kitson at the Wolverhampton office where they both worked. Brown, an insurance executive, wrote in her notebook 'I want to make love to you'. The industrial tribunal, which met in August 1989, also heard how he fondled Mrs Kitson intimately and stroked her leg in front of a client; pulled her into an office and put his arms around her; stroked her neck and let his hand stray to her chest; suggested having an affair and pushed himself against her; said he could help 'if she was lonely'.

On other occasions, she said, Brown would run his hands up her leg behind the office counter while they were talking to clients, and once he touched her while she was on the telephone. She said he had also proposed 'business trips' which turned out to be schemes for going for a meal and then to a hotel. She stayed with the firm as long as she could because she was a single parent with a seven-year-old son and did not want to live on social security. Later she left because she could stand it no longer. Brown denied the allegations, claiming Mrs Kitson had been under pressure because of her insurance examinations. He insisted that nothing of a sexual nature had taken place and that he was a happily married man.

The 'happiness' of married men, however, does not prevent them becoming sex pests at work, particularly when divorced or separated women are concerned. It does not prevent them humiliating a woman subordinate by saying and doing embarrassing things to her in the company of outsiders, knowing that she will be reluctant to complain. Such men prey on the vulnerability of the woman who needs the cash to bring up her family, thinking she is more likely to be compliant if she is worried about her job prospects.

Tribunal chairman Bernard Owens took the view that Mrs Kitson had not imagined it. He said: 'She did not dream this up. Her evidence is acceptable to us.' He said Mrs Kitson had immediately told her agency of the situation and that is not what someone dreaming in a fantasy world would do.

Mrs Kitson was awarded £500 for injury to her feelings and £1,394 for loss of earnings as a result of Brown's harassment. She described the verdict as 'absolutely fantastic' but added that she was 'still very, very, angry. The money will not really compensate for the emotional trauma I have been through.'

After the hearing Brown put his jacket over his head to avoid being photographed and left without talking to the press. Brown, presumably, kept his job while Mrs Kitson was forced to leave hers.

What justice was that? The 'absolutely fantastic' verdict — her words — would not have paid her bills for long.

My own view is that women will soon regard such a verdict as unjust, that the compensation was in no way commensurate with the crime. Indeed, the day is dawning when women like Carolyn Kitson will not need to leave their job at all.

THREE

POWER OVER WOMEN

Sexual harassment is a manifestation of male domination over women, as dozens of industrial tribunal cases constantly remind us.

However, some women who have made it to the top of their particular career ladder find they are still vulnerable to the attentions of the kind of man who wants to 'keep them down' or destabilise them in their jobs.

Brenda Dean, General Secretary of the print union SOGAT, suffered her first, and only, experience of sexual harassment long after she had achieved power in her union. She was taken completely by surprise because she had assumed, not unnaturally, that she would encounter such treatment on the way up the trade union ladder, not *after* she had reached the summit. The incident happened in a fashionable restaurant near the famous Connaught Rooms, off London's Kingsway. Miss Dean, breaking off negotiations with employers, joined a middle-aged bachelor director and two others for dinner.

During the meal the man started fondling her thigh. At first she ignored it because, as many women will confirm, she just could not believe it was happening. She had done nothing to encourage him, tease him, or deliberately interest him. They were, after all, discussing how they could attain a satisfactory settlement for her members employed by a printing company in the South. Miss Dean says she was angry, very angry, and felt 'shocked'. The man soon realised he had bitten off more than he could chew on this occasion. He foolishly repeated his action, which most harassers do, and this time Miss Dean knew it was no accident.

She stopped eating, told him firmly and politely what to do with himself, and warned him that she would walk out of the restaurant if he persisted. The man, she says, was acutely flustered and embarrassed, as were the two other diners.

The working dinner ended without further incident. But she was in no mood to let him off the hook. Months later they met again, and he told her that he had just been married. 'Perhaps you will stop touching other women's legs from now on,' she told him. Miss Dean said: 'What annoyed me most of all was the arrogant manner in which it was done. The fact that he felt he could do that and get away with it. There was certainly no intellectual build up, smooth chat or anything of that sort. He got his come-uppance and I hope he has started behaving himself.'

Although she has won a deserved reputation as a hard and shrewd negotiator, Miss Dean says she still has to put up with a 'lot of male nonsense'. One day, at a reception, she asked for a glass of sherry. A man said: 'If you are doing a man's job why don't you have a man's drink?' She told him: 'If that is your mental attitude you will be easy meat in negotiations.' She said later: 'He just shrivelled before my eyes.'

Miss Dean admits that she is in a position of relative power and authority not enjoyed by a female shop floor factory worker. She says: 'I can get away with it but I feel desperately sorry for women who feel they have to take that sort of behaviour.' It is time, says Miss Dean, for women workers to assert themselves and refuse to be intimidated by men who want to 'put them down'. She will not allow men to get away with foul and abusive language in her presence. On the rare occasion anyone swears in her company she asks them, politely, to desist. 'For some reason some men like to swear in the presence of women and believe you have got to accept it. Well I don't and I make sure they apologise.'

Brenda Dean thus joins the statistics which show that

at least one woman in ten has suffered harassment at work.

Actress Justine Kerrigan, who plays Tracy Corkhill in television's *Brookside*, said it was alarming simply to play the part of a girl being harassed. In *Woman* magazine Miss Kerrigan, then nineteen, said she trembled when reading the script and felt 'awkward and embarrassed' when confronted by a sweating, heavy-breathing would-be seducer who had power over her. He was the oily boss of the hairdressing salon where she worked. She played the part of just the kind of girl Brenda Dean feels sorry for — a helpless teenager, desperate for job security and a living wage, confronted by a lecherous man with sexual demands and the power of hire-and-fire. Miss Kerrigan told the magazine: 'I felt ashamed and nervous when we had to be physically close. Then I thought: "If you want to carry on with an acting career you're going to have to do worse than this." But I was relieved once the scene was over.' *Brookside* did its seven million weekly viewers a favour. Probably for the first time on television the subject of sexual harassment was treated as a serious social problem and not a seedy joke.

Tracy Corkhill was finally sacked, days before Christmas, on the flimsy pretext that she had been late for work. Like many women who suffer this form of harassment in real life, she took the case to a tribunal.

Miss Kerrigan told journalist Val Sampson: 'It must be terrifying. Girls who suffer like Tracy feel so helpless. When your job is on the line you are scared to say anything. But a man has no right to do that. I can imagine that an experience like that would put you off men altogether.' The letters poured into the television studio, proving that the subject had struck a nerve among many armchair fans. Unlike her screen character, Miss Kerrigan said she was sure she could handle sexual harassment if she had to. She added: 'I wouldn't let anyone take advantage of me in any way. The best thing to do is to tell someone. I'd tell my dad because I know he would understand, and handle it properly.' Producer Vanessa Whitburn summed up: 'Justine is one of our best people on the team. Tracy is growing up and learning about the world. And if just one of the men who might harass a woman stops doing it, we have done the best thing drama can do.'

The question of power is taken up by a campaigning organisation called WASH — Women Against Sexual Harassment — which looks after and counsels the victims of sex pests. Its belief is that the harasser, if found guilty, should be dismissed from his job, or at the very least suspended and transferred to another area. WASH, which operates from a little office near London's King's Cross, has had up to 300 cases on its books at one time. The cases all involve women workers needing help from the misery inflicted by bosses and workmates — all men. Valerie Mainstone, the 'support clinic's' only full-time employee, leads an unpaid team of eighteen women who assist victims.

Valerie, herself a victim who has changed jobs to escape the unwanted attentions of harassers, is in no doubt why men sexually harass women. She said: 'It is power, the power men traditionally and historically have over women. It is men who must behave and change their ways. Women have modified their behaviour and dress over the centuries to accommodate men and can do no more. Harassment ruins careers and job prospects and leads to a variety of illnesses among women workers. If men cannot learn to behave correctly they must be dismissed. This is an issue which dates back centuries but one which must be discussed openly and cannot be ignored any longer.'

WASH was founded in 1985 and does not keep statistics. 'We are here to help people and maintain confidentiality, we are not a library of stats,' explained Valerie. WASH is not against men and women being friendly to each other or calling each other 'pet names', so long as this does not cause offence to the recipient. Even praising a girl's hair or her dress may not be acceptable, stresses Valerie. She said: 'It is a delicate area and a man must think very carefully before he comments on a woman's appearance. His comments may not be appreciated and this in itself is a mild form of harassment. Would a man tell his boss that his hair and his suit look nice? Why should a boss tell his secretary "Get me a cup of tea, pet" when she has to say "Yes, Mr Brown"?' She added: 'It is this attitude towards women which undermines their place in society and the work environment.'

Valerie refuses to criticise Page-3 girls or any woman who is employed as a pin-up. She said: 'I would never criticise a woman on an individual basis because women have always been exploited by men in this way. It is the whole process which helps to undermine the role of working women.' Industrial tribunals are regularly used by women who have complained about their treatment by male colleagues. Valerie added: 'Why is it the woman who is transferred or suspended, or even sacked, after complaining about being sexually attacked or harassed? If a man complains that his wallet has been stolen by a colleague he is never sent home in disgrace prior to a hearing. It is the thief who is sent home.'

WASH says men should realise that comments about physical appearance, particularly size of breasts, are often unwanted and unreciprocated. Unnecessary touching and sexual innuendos are harassment and such behaviour should be illegal. Valerie argues: 'There is hardly a job where women are immune from sexual harassment. Our experience is that women have no further need to restructure their dress or behaviour. No matter what their dress, colour, race or religion, they will be the subject of abuse, particularly by men in positions of power. It has existed ever since men and women started working together, but that is no excuse for assault and there is no reason why women should have to accept it. The very word harassment implies that women have got to put up with a lot, but once is too often.'

A typical case, says WASH, is the man who abuses his power by harassing women who are generally in subordinate roles. The victim's first reaction should be to tell him that his remarks and attentions are not welcome, and, if necessary, female colleagues and union officials should be informed. Valerie said: 'If women ignore it and the problem does not go away, it invariably gets worse. The result is that women often leave their jobs. I know one woman who left her job three times because of it.'

Employers have a duty, says WASH, to ensure that the workplace is a healthy and safe environment for everybody. 'We are not killjoys, we want people to be nice to each other, but we want to change the climate of opinion. Things which were once said a few years ago about race are not said today because opinions have changed. Women want harassment to end, and end quickly. Women should get the support of their colleagues, friends and relatives because there is safety in numbers and this assistance gives them confidence. Male colleagues of the victim can help a great deal by stopping the pest. For too long men have stood by, themselves too ashamed to do anything about it.'

Valerie Mainstone added: 'In the real world the cards are stacked against women. A man spurned at the office can put the boot into a woman in a conversation at his golf club and she has no way of knowing why she lost the job.'

No man ever admits to sexual harassment. To them, it is something which other men do to other women, or something which exists only in somebody's mind. Perhaps some of them are so conceited they are oblivious to the feelings of others and do not even realise they are doing it. Some women are very frank when the subject of harassment is raised, although many victims hide behind a weak smile and suffer in silence. Christine Garbutt, a colleague at the *Daily Mirror*, told me how she endured unwanted attention in her early days in journalism. I found her account particularly moving, because no male colleague to my knowledge has ever had to tolerate this kind of behaviour in his quest to succeed in journalism.

Christine said: 'I do not believe a girl reaches the age of eighteen without having experienced sexual harassment of one form or another. Maybe she doesn't recognise it as that. In common parlance it is "bloody men". In its mild form sexual harassment is not easy to define. Some women object to a wolf whistle in the street, others dislike all men who call them "dear" or "love". I suspect I am in the majority when I say what is acceptable, even nice from one man, is instinctively threatening and abhorrent from another. Most offices have at least one man who is a male chauvinist pig.

'The lewd, crude, macho man who pats you on the bum, feels at liberty to mention your "tits", whose conversation, if you can call it that, is littered with sexual innuendos. There is only one way to deal with the pest. Look him straight in the eye and tell him where to get off, and mean it. Loudly if you like. Make him feel small. Girls should be taught this by their mothers, or at school. Sadly, sexual harassment is never on the curriculum. Much worse, and I suspect it happens far more often than we know, is physical sexual harassment where the girl agrees to it, because she feels her job would be at risk if she refuses. The younger the girl, the more worried she would be. Who does she tell? What should she do? She doesn't want a scene, besides she knows her job would more likely be on the line than his.

'The first time this happened to me I was seventeen years old, working as a junior reporter on a local paper. I was covering an evening event: the editor was there. He offered me a lift home to my digs. It did not occur to me that I was less than safe with this "God" in his mid-fifties. He stopped the car a few doors down from where I was living. I went to get out. Suddenly the door was slammed shut. I was thrown on the seat, mauled and kissed. I tried to fend him off, his hands grappled at my pants. "Stop, stop," I cried, unable to believe what was happening. I was kicking and slapping him. He did stop, and I ran out. That night I was sick. I did not dare tell my mother because she would have gone round to the office and caused a scene. I could not cope with that.

'I was sure I would lose my job. I just wanted to disappear, wishing desperately it had never happened. In a state of anxiety I reported for work. After half an hour the editor called me in. I was sure he was going to give me my cards. Instead, he asked me brusquely to cover a story. He looked me menacingly in the eye. I got the unspoken message "you say nothing and we will forget the incident". Women cannot forget these incidents. No more can I forget the time when, years later, when I was working at another newspaper, we held a dance. The managing director was there. He was eyeing me up and I was flattered until he came over and pushed me into a corner. "Does your husband lick your ... the way I could?" he said. My horrified reaction was to push him away and he fell, knocking over chairs and tables. I expected the sack. Again, nothing occurred.

'When I had children I went freelance. A new editor arrived at one of the papers I had been working for for a decade. He was the one whose advances I had put off years ago. He soon called me in. "Christine, we won't be commissioning your work but we still want you to write for us. Shall we lunch to discuss it?" He was leering at me. Old scores would be settled. He knew I was the sole breadwinner in the family. It was bed or nothing. I chose nothing. Men say that women flaunt themselves in offices, and wear too short, too tight, unsuitable clothes for the office. "They ask for it," they say. But no woman wants to be degraded in this way. We don't want dirty talk, we don't want to be groped and mauled.

'And if we are, we want to know exactly what to do and where to go, without fear of repercussions. But how do you legislate for that?'

There can be no better, or worse, example of a boss abusing his power over women workers than the case of frozen fish company boss Michael Alway, fifty-three, who hit the headlines in April 1989, when two former employees branded him a sex pest. The girls were low-paid workers, hundreds of miles from home, and anxious to earn a living. Alway used his position to seek sexual favours but only ended up making himself look a laughing stock while making the girls' lives a misery. Brian Walton, Chairman of the industrial tribunal, held at Exeter, said Alway was guilty of "galloping carnality". Power at work Alway clearly had aplenty. Charisma he had not.

The two angry young women told how they were harassed out of their jobs. The *Sun* newspaper, under the headline '£6,000 Bill Puts Randy Fish Boss in His Plaice' may have reported the case accurately but, I suspect, failed to record the anguish felt by these two women at being hounded out of their careers. The *Sun*, running true to form, could not resist describing them as 'lovely', 'attractive', 'pretty', and 'buxom'.

The two women were Elisa Loveless, twenty-four, of Plymouth, Devon, and Marnie Stinson, twenty-two, of Scarborough, Yorks. Marnie said Alway's behaviour forced her to leave her job as a linguist with his L'Amiral seafood firm, while Elisa said she was fired as £12,000-a-year operations manager for Alway's Flow International food distribution company in Plymouth after refusing his advances.

The tribunal heard how Alway offered to increase Marnie's salary, help buy her a flat, and take her to Gibraltar. Marnie said the bearded, balding boss told her: 'You make things happen in my trousers' and 'I like your skirt, it shows off your backside'. His attempts at seducing Elisa had similar charm. He is alleged to have said: 'My thing throbs when I see you', and he described her bosoms as 'big, juicy boobs'.

Marine said that shortly after she started work Alway invited her out to dinner. She told the tribunal: 'His whole conversation revolved around sex. He told me details about his experiences at wife-swapping parties.' On their return home he stopped the car and stroked her leg. She added: 'He would not pay me my proper salary of £8,000 a year unless I went to bed with him.' Elisa was awarded £2,600 in damages and back pay for sexual harassment, while Marine received £2,000. Alway was also ordered to pay £1,250 costs. Elisa, described by the *Daily Star* as a 'stunning blonde', said the final straw came when Alway booked a double room in a London hotel when they went to an exhibition at Billingsgate. She told him to sleep in his car, caused a scene, and found herself a single room. She says she was fired after just three months. She added: 'I felt Mike Alway, having tried in vain, sacked me because I would not have a sexual relationship with him.'

The women obviously gained some consolation, even vengeance, from the embarrassing publicity dished out to Alway, although it took courage on their part to take the case to a tribunal in the first place.

But Alway remained in highly-paid employment, while they remained dismissed. *Daily Mirror* writer Mary Riddell summed the tribunal up in an article, 'How to Trap the Office Sex Pest'. She wrote: 'Michael Alway is the classic example of the office sex pest. Balding, unlikely to be mistaken for Robert Redford, and blessed with the sort of bushy beard which looks as if it has the remains of breakfast egg stuck in it. In short, a man with about as much charisma as one of the frozen dinners he marketed from the premises where he entertained his female employees with his delightful line in office small-talk. Let us not dwell too much on the collected sayings of Mr Alway, nicknamed "Mr Thingy", for obvious reasons, after the evidence given by his two employees, Elisa Loveless and Marnie Stinson. Suffice it to say that his best lines included "Turn around so that I can see your backside" and "Things are moving inside my trousers". It is hard to imagine the trauma that these women must have endured in their fight to bring this thoroughly nasty little man to book. This week they must have rejoiced, not just for their victory but for the knowledge that it will encourage other women to try to take their cases to industrial tribunals.'

Fiona Fox, of the Equal Opportunities Commission, told Mary: 'It marks a big step forward. Every time a case like this is reported we hear of more complaints. There is also a move up in the amount of damages being paid. One thousand pounds is now the minimum for sexual harassment cases whereas, in other sex discrimination cases, it is the maximum figure.'

Mary reported that, in spite of the breakthrough, the number of complaints is probably tiny compared with the number of offences. Said Fiona Fox: 'It is the tip of the iceberg. The onus is still on women to provide the proof of what has happened to them, and no woman is going to enjoy the prospect of standing in front of a court and being questioned.' Mary Riddell said: 'Surveys have shown that half of women who work have suffered the attentions of the office sex pest. Yet last year only 150 complained to the Equal Opportunities Commission.'

There are plenty of Michael Always about, warned Mary, and said the 'typical sex pest tends to run to a type. He is less likely to be Kevin from accounts, suffering from terminal acne and a dangerous overdose of the Brut aftershave his auntie gave him for Christmas, than someone in the Alway mould.' Warming to her theme Mary got it spot on: 'He is likely to be a self-employed creep, running his own small business with a pleasant sideline in seduction techniques. Other groups have been singled out — Oxford dons, driving instructors. What they have in common is that they all see themselves as dominant, powerful men. The boss. And when they get found out, they have a way of disappearing into the woodwork. More and more men are keeping their cases secret by persuading women to sign no-publicity clauses as a condition of out-of-court settlements.

'This means the likes of Mr Alway can continue their biology lessons without the details being splashed all over the newspapers.'

Two different lessons emerged from the Alway case. The first was summed up by Elisa Loveless: 'No woman should have to put up with this sort of treatment.' The second is that there are only two ways to beat men like him. To complain. And to fight.

Lessons apart, however, the psychological effects on the victims in this case, as in similar cases, were profound. Marnie Stinson told journalist Caro Thompson, writing for a woman's magazine, about her experiences working for Michael Alway. She said: 'After months of searching I'd landed what sounded like the perfect job. I was so excited. It was in Plymouth, which meant moving down from York, where I lived, but that was exactly what I wanted, a brand new start. And I'd be much nearer my boyfriend who was in the Navy and based in Cornwall.

'I was twenty-two and it was my second job. I was longing to use the bilingual secretarial course I'd done at college. I'd been interviewed by three men, all directors of a brand new import/export company handling seafoods. I'd be in from the start, helping to get the company off the ground.

'They seemed to like me, everything was friendly and I was thrilled when the boss, Mike, rang to offer me the job. He was grey-haired, in his fifties, married with two children, and he seemed charming. Mike promised me a good salary and I looked forward to showing him just how hard I could work and helping him to build up his new business.

'He did ask me a few slightly strange questions, such as whether I had a boyfriend. But I honestly didn't think too much about it. I just assumed he wanted to make sure I wouldn't leave too soon to start a family. I worked in a nice office with another girl, Lisa, and I was responsible for trying to set up business for the company. I worked really hard, staying late and going in at weekends too.

'After a couple of weeks Mike, who didn't work in the office with us, offered to take me out to dinner. He seemed concerned because I didn't know anyone in the area yet. He was kind and fatherly and seemed to want to make sure I was all right. I happily accepted. But the minute we got into his car he changed totally. He started talking about sex, wife-swapping parties and how attractive I was. I was absolutely stunned. I kept trying politely to steer the conversation on to other things.

'It carried on all through dinner. Then he said he'd drive me home. It was a few minutes before I realised we were heading the wrong way. We got to an area where it was totally dark and he pulled into a clearing. I kept telling myself to keep calm, but I was terrified. I thought he was going to rape me and I didn't know whether to get out and run.

'He grabbed my hand and started touching my leg. Trying to sound very calm I asked him to take me home. Eventually he did, saying he hoped I wasn't offended but he really wanted to go to bed with me. If it had been anyone but my boss I'd have yelled at him, but I felt I couldn't — I didn't want to lose my job.

'I told him I was offended and that I didn't believe in mixing business with pleasure. He knew I had a serious boyfriend and I made it clear I wasn't interested in him. Over the next few weeks, he never stopped pestering me. He would come round to my flat in the evenings, pretending he wanted to discuss work. I used to leave the light off and refuse to answer the door.

'But he got round that by phoning me from his car, telling me he'd be arriving in a couple of minutes. Sometimes he'd come twice in an evening, or at the weekend. I told my boyfriend, but we only saw each other every second weekend and so there wasn't much he could do. He was furious and wanted to go and confront Mike but I asked him not to. I was afraid it might jeopardise my job. I thought I could cope with it all by myself.

'Mike would talk about sex, making jokes and innuendos all the time. He would try to get me to bend over by the filing cabinets when he came into my office. I told him I thought he was disgusting and pathetic. He'd just laugh and say I liked it really, and that eventually I'd change my mind about going to bed with him.

'One day I felt at the end of my tether and I told Lisa. She said he'd been doing it to her too. We became friends and I felt at least I had some support. But a few weeks later Mike asked Lisa to leave. He replaced her with a man, so I was the only girl left. I decided to move in with Lisa, but Mike said he wouldn't employ me if I did.

'The final blow came when I realised he was only paying me about two thirds of the salary he'd promised. I confronted him and he laughed, saying he'd never promised to pay me that much. But he said he'd help me buy a flat if we had a closer relationship. I walked out and never went back. I cried and cried. Five months after starting my dream job my life seemed to be in ruins. That same week my boyfriend and I split up and I'm sure it was because I'd been under so much constant pressure.

'I felt my life had fallen to pieces. No job, no boyfriend, a long way from home and all because of that awful man. My confidence was rock bottom. I'd always been relaxed and comfortable in men's company before. Now I felt I couldn't trust anyone, or anything men said to me. I stayed in Plymouth for a couple of months doing temp jobs. Then I went back to live with my parents in Scarborough. I felt it was better to start all over again.

'But, before I left, Lisa and I wrote down all that had happened to us and decided to try to do something about it. I went to a solicitor, and he told me we'd got a strong case of sexual harassment. He got in touch with the Equal Opportunities Commission and they said they'd pay all our expenses. That was wonderful as we were both stony broke and you can't get legal aid for a tribunal. Our case came up in Exeter, six months afterwards. Waiting for it was hard.

'I would have crying fits for hours. I'd so wanted to succeed in that job. And I dreaded going over it all again in court. My family was very supportive although my dad was furious of course. The case took two days. Mike's solicitor grilled me about whether I'd led Mike on. I got so angry I shouted at him because he kept twisting my words. But we won. I was awarded £2,000 for emotional upset and loss of earnings.

'I don't know whether I'll ever see the money, though. We're having to take more legal action to get it. A lot of women said "good for you" when they heard about the case.

'After I appeared in our local paper some women came up to me in the street and said "well done" and that made me feel much better. I felt proud then and glad it meant something to people. I'm working in a bookshop now but I'm hoping to get another job where I can use my languages and perhaps move away from home and get a flat again.

'I'm definitely very cautious about men now. I'm more careful about how I react. I know teasing and flirting goes on in every workplace and I used to enjoy that. It's quite different from what Mike did to me. I felt he ruined my life. Well, I'm picking it up again now.

'But I'll never, never forget.'

Dorothy Wade, writing in *The Sunday Times* on 23 April, 1989, said that many women must have experienced a 'vicarious sense of revenge' when the two female managers, Elisa Loveless and Marnie Stinson, won their sexual harassment case against their sex pest boss Mike Alway. She felt, however, that their damages were 'derisory' while Alway continued in his job. She said this was 'scant compensation for their lost jobs and anguish' and that definitions of sexual harassment were 'vague', with many women afraid to complain because of 'coercion' on the part of the harasser, who is usually someone in a senior position to the victim.

Wade was pleased, however, that such victories

reflected an increasing recognition that sexual harassment can be dealt with in the courts. She pointed out that, until the 1980s, no sexual harassment cases were brought and quoted an employment lawyer, Denise Kingsmill, as saying: 'It used to be regarded as part of the rough and tumble of working life.' Wade also pointed out that, as women are fast becoming more confident about bringing harassment into the open, men 'appear to find it a confusing subject. When raised, men often treat it as a joke. Perhaps they are unsure of how their behaviour is construed by their female colleagues. Many are not sure when they are crossing the fine line between friendly chat and becoming a pest.'

She added: 'Most women can cope with the odd tasteless remark (although they would prefer not to have to). But serious problems arise when these escalate into more unpleasant behaviour: the woman becomes aware that the man is mentally "undressing her"; a caressing hand appears too often on her shoulder or even her leg; eventually there may be the ultimate threat that the victim will be sacked if she doesn't consent to sex.' Wade says that even if such harassment does not lead to a woman's dismissal by a frustrated boss, it frequently results in her depression and lost confidence. Fortunately, this grave problem is receiving increasing recognition. Employers, realising that sexual harassment can lead to the loss of valuable staff and also to hefty pay-offs, are introducing codes of practice, providing channels of complaint, and in some cases, dismissing violators. She continues that a 'firm letter from a group of women cataloguing a colleague's offences may be all that is needed to stop him.' Denise Kingsmill believes that such developments are leading to a social change which is essential. She argues: 'We need to get to the stage where men are ashamed to behave like that, where it is seen as offensive, not only by women but by their male colleagues, too. We need men to be offended by the slur such behaviour casts on them.'

*

A shock survey by *The Times* showed that one in ten female undergraduates at Cambridge University suffers unwanted sexual attention from dons, and more than one third have been subjected to unsolicited advances from other students. Higher Education reporter Sam Kiley said that 1 per cent of women who responded to the Cambridge University Student Union survey said they had been raped by fellow students, while another 2.7 per cent reported 'sexual aggression'. Researchers found that 10 per cent of respondents reported some form of sexual attention from supervisors, mostly in the form of 'unwanted suggestive looks', 'being eyed up and down' and 'sexual remarks/jokes'. The survey, reported in *The Times* on 1 June, 1989, was sent to university administrators and women's officers in each college. It said that almost 2 per cent of women reported requests for dates or sex, unwanted cheek kissing, touching and grabbing, by tutors.

Miss Claire Steedman, Women's Officer of the union and a first-year student at New Hall, said that although the women's council of the union, which organised the survey, had attempted to send questionnaires to all the 3,000 to 4,000 women attending the university, they were disappointed that only 776 replied. She said that at one college, which had agreed to admit women, only fourteen questionnaires were returned and many had been filled in with bogus information. Obscene items were also posted in the collection box.

After a similar survey into sexual harassment at Oxford University, the results of which were kept secret, Kiley reported that the Hebdomadal Council, the university's governing body, ordered that a code of conduct be circulated to all colleges and a disciplinary framework be set up to deal with complaints. He said no such system existed at Cambridge, but that the student union hoped to maintain its annual survey of the extent of the problem.

The survey found that 55 per cent of women felt they could not report incidents of harassment to a college fellow, while, surprisingly, 54 per cent said they could not report incidents to the union. Only 7 per cent said that they felt the university could deal effectively with their problems. One third of the respondents said their work had suffered through harassment which, they said, was frequently the result of drunkenness. Kiley reported that students had the worst record for harassing women — 25.3 per cent of whom reported unwanted touching and grabbing from their peers. In addition, 2.7 per cent, or twenty-one women, said they had been victims of 'forcible aggression'. Seven women, or 1 per cent, said they had been raped by students.

The report was also critical of academics' attitudes to women in the classroom. Miss Bonnie Scarborough, author of the report and Women's Officer at St Edmund's College, said 'supervisors and lecturers had less time for women.

'Some teachers had trouble relating to women and ignored them instead.' She said that 'some women reported that supervisors and lecturers made sexist remarks and were patronising, and assumed that they were stupid if they were attractive.' Dr David Bruce, Senior Tutor at Corpus Christi, and Secretary of the Senior Tutors' Representative Council, said the university was aware of the problems facing female students. However, he said the changes in attitudes would have to start at college level. 'There is evidence in my observations of the relationship between women students and their supervisors that among some dons there is a lingering attitude that women are not really serious about study — that is an attitude we are trying to eliminate.'

Oxford: The harassment of students by dons had resulted in an 'historic victory' for women at Oxford, according to *The Sunday Telegraph*'s Charles Oulton on 5 June, 1988.

He said that, after years of ignoring complaints about male tutors harassing their female undergraduates, the Hebdomadal Council, an administrative body, had agreed to a review of the ways in which an academic relationship can become more than just an hour-long tutorial. He said that Sir John Walton, Warden of Green College and President of the General Medical Council, would begin testing allegations against male Fellows by both women undergraduates and women tutors. The inquiry followed the questioning, in 1987, of a don at Pembroke College, who has now given up teaching. He was alleged to have made one undergraduate pregnant and to have tried to seduce other students. He was also alleged to have told them that they could fail their exams if they did not give in to his demands, which often reduced women students to tears. The decision to hold an inquiry, according to the *Daily Mail* on 13 June, 1988, followed a string of complaints against the tutor and claims of offences by others, including rape and an enforced abortion.

Liz Lightfoot, Education Correspondent of the *Mail on Sunday*, reported on 19 February, 1989 that Oxford, as a result of the inquiry, would set out a code of conduct banning physical or sexual behaviour of an 'unwanted and inappropriate nature' by dons. It also established councillors and advisory councils in the colleges to hear complaints and required the university and faculties to set up a confidential appeals system. Lightfoot quoted Professor Ralf Dahrendorf, Warden of St Anthony's, the first college to set up an advisory council on sexual harassment: 'We must find a way of making women students feel safe.' Sarah Ross, President of the Junior Common Room at St Anthony's College, told Lightfoot: 'This is a very reactionary and male-dominated university. Some colleges have been unwilling to accept strong words for the code because they just don't recognise the problem. When women have complained in the past it has all been brushed under the carpet because the dons are all very well known and are valuable to the colleges.'

Gym mistress Liz Davaney, twenty-seven, resigned her job and claimed constructive dismissal after complaining that married schoolmaster Chris Stone, thirty-one, harassed her during her eight-month stay at Ousedale School, Newport Pagnell. She claimed he hugged and kissed her.

The case prompted Jane Adams, of the *Today* newspaper, to seek guidance from psychologist Glenn Wilson, who said the serious sex pest 'is quite incapable of seeing he has crossed the line from social banter to blatant sexual harassment. He cannot take "no" for an answer.' Dr Wilson added: 'The lecher is socially inept and doesn't realise he is following an outdated courtship ritual. It is not only traditional but biological in most species that the man is expected to be the pursuer. He would normally expect his persistence to be rewarded by the woman.

'Men like this tend to believe that a woman worth some trouble might be some trouble. So he might persist on the basis that he might break through that resistance. More often he has miscalculated and does not realise she is just not interested.'

Dr Wilson said the serious sex pest is often married, which makes his harassment even more abhorrent.

National Union of Teachers: A document published by the NUT concentrated specifically on schools where the 'workplace' involves children as well as adults. It said that, although the guidelines are addressed to teachers in schools, it is recognised that their contents have a relevance for teachers in other educational establishments. It says the union hopes that the guidelines offer practical advice and establish a climate which discourages sexual harassment. But the document admits: 'It is obviously impossible to lay down guidelines to cover all eventualities.' Who is affected?

'Although, on occasion, men and boys may experience sexual harassment, the majority of those who suffer this form of victimisation are women and girls. This is hardly surprising, as sexual harassment stems from the abuse of power, where men play a dominating role in society.

'Schools are rather different from other work environments because both children and adults are present. The possibility of additional kinds of sexual harassment is consequently greater: teachers or ancillary staff, or other persons present on the school premises, may be responsible for harassing pupils, while pupils may be responsible for harassing adults. Because teachers have a pastoral responsibility for their pupils, they have a particular concern where pupils are involved in any way in harassment.

'Professional good sense should help the teacher to avoid situations which could lead to accusations of sexual harassment, although it has to be recognised that interpretations of what constitutes harassment differ and that what is accepted as friendliness by one person may well be interpreted as unwelcome attention by another.'

The NUT says that sexual harassment of teacher or pupil is unprofessional conduct within the terms of the union's Code of Professional Conduct and advises members on the role of the union's divisions in dealing with it. Again, a model clause for education authorities suggests that the harassers, and not victims, should be relocated.

Individual members are advised that they should 'never intentionally' behave in a way which could be regarded as harassment. The document's guidelines say: 'You should constantly examine your behaviour towards others at school and within the union to make sure that your behaviour and language cannot be construed as harassment.'

Victims are advised:

'It is important to make it clear as soon as possible that such behaviour is unacceptable and violates an agreed code of practice.

'If the harassment continues, and your harasser is a colleague, you should bring the situation to the attention of the Head with a view to invoking the grievance procedure.

'The support of the school representative (NUT) may also be sought. Should the situation remain unresolved, you should get in touch with an officer of your local association, the executive member in your area, or your regional official, with a view to their taking up the matter on your behalf. At the same time, you should inform the Head that you have taken this step.

'If the harasser is your Headteacher, again in the context of invoking the grievance procedure, you should bring the situation immediately to the attention of an officer of your local association, the executive member of your area, or your regional official, with a view to their taking up the matter on your behalf.

'If the harasser is also a union member, you may finally decide to make a formal complaint to the union on the grounds of unprofessional conduct. The complaint will then be processed under the established professional conduct procedure of the union.

'If your harasser is neither a teacher nor a pupil but is another employee of the local authority, or any person present on the school premises, you should, in the first instance, bring the matter to the attention of the Head and proceed as advised above.

'If you are being harassed by a pupil, it may be unwise to deal with the matter directly. You should seek the advice of the Headteacher.

'If the matter remains unresolved, you may wish to pursue the case through appropriate union channels.'

Union representatives are advised to encourage victims to note details of each occurrence of harassment and monitor any changes in the attitude of the harasser towards the victim. This information could be useful in countering any subsequent attempts at victimisation, or any attack on professional incompetence. The guidelines state: 'It is essential to recognise that reporting sexual harassment can isolate the victim and lead to increased victimisation. Therefore, cases need to be handled sensitively, not only because of that possibility but also because it is vital to ensure that members are not afraid of reporting cases, and that they are given support and help once they have reported their problem, by both the union and by those with whom they work.'

Regarding pupil harassment, the guidelines stress that, because of their immaturity, children and young people are vulnerable targets for harassment. The union warns: 'In addition, they will not have a union to support them in defending their rights, so that it is essential that a pupil who is the victim of harassment should feel able to approach a teacher for help and advice in tackling the problem.

'As a teacher, you clearly have a responsibility to support and assist pupils who experience sexual harassment, either from other pupils or from teaching or ancillary staff, or from any person present on the school premises.'

Members are advised that if they witness the harassment of a pupil, or if a pupil complains about being harassed, they should take steps to prevent its continuation or recurrence by making full use of any existing policy/code of practice. 'You should, in any case, report the matter immediately to the Head. It may also be advisable for the school to involve the relevant sector of the local education authority, such as the Educational Welfare Service, in accordance with procedures established by the authority.'

My brother unions are not blameless and I have encountered many cases of sexism and patriarchal attitudes. The use of women as sex symbols is not the monopoly of big business, advertising and girlie mag publishers. For example, miners' leader Arthur Scargill and former *Yorkshire Miner* editor Maurice Jones both supported the use of pin-ups in the *Yorkshire Miner* newspaper. Scargill has never apologised but, for Jones, it is a time for repentance. Bathing costumes, never nudity, were the order of the day in the *Yorkshire Miner* and only the relatives of miners were used on page three to give the paper a 'coal community flavour'. They justified the use of 'glamour pictures' on the grounds that miners were attracted to the capitalist press by such pictures. As a result Scargill and Jones were accused of sexism. The feminists regarded it as a blatant, crude, pathetic excuse to boost circulation by capitalist press methods.

Jones said: 'The editor of *Coal News*, the National Coal Board paper, once told me he wished he had thought of the idea himself.' Jones, forty-six, and the father of a sixteen-year-old daughter, is now a twisted soul on the delicate subject of pin-ups, a blatant exploitation of women. When I raised the matter with him he said: 'Oh, no. This will always come back to haunt me.' He and Scargill were savaged by a female audience during a debate in London and 'King' Arthur was called upon to justify the use of such pictures. He wisely ordered Jones to join him for moral support. Jones said: 'Those were different days, a very different climate.

'I told people, miners included, that it was necessary to fight Fleet Street techniques with similar strategy. If miners enjoyed looking at the *Daily Mirror* or the *Sun* because of pin-ups they would buy the *Yorkshire Miner* for the same reason. I must admit I made a mistake in going to London with Scargill that day for the debate. I told the audience that there was a feminist mafia about wearing dishevelled jackets and dungarees, that the women had no sense of humour. I was lucky to escape with my unmentionables intact. They went absolutely barmy. Later, at a Communist Party reception a woman glowered at me and threw a cup of coffee in my direction. She accused me of "oppressing" her by publishing pictures of pretty women in bathing costumes or bikinis. The format, however, was a success and the paper was described as the liveliest union paper in the business.

'I published such photographs for five years, from 1977 to 1982. The last picture was a nurse in uniform, not a pin-up. My successor dropped the glamour pictures and there is no evidence of the circulation falling because he got rid of them. Women of all ages, as well as men, praised me for the pictures, saying, "What's wrong with a pretty pit lass in the paper?" Ultra left-wingers, however, gave me a hard time over it. Looking back, I do not think I would repeat the exercise. Now I have a teenage daughter of my own, I realise just how women are exploited, pigeon-holed and stereotyped by men. I did not fully realise it at the time.

'The *Guardian* did a profile on me and the *Yorkshire Miner* and gave me a rough ride. They said I was "100 per cent Groucho and 30 per cent Karl". I suppose I deserved it.

'It was necessary to build up the circulation figures of the paper at that critical time in its history and circulation grew as a result. In all fairness I have to admit that there was not a flood of protests when they stopped. Nowadays I see clearly how such pictures can be offensive to women and that such exploitation of the female body has gone on for a millennium. I felt I was doing the right thing at the time, but the climate of opinion would not allow it today. Now I am much more sensitive to the feelings of women.'

*

Women are not even safe from the attentions of harassers on public transport, as we see all too frequently from criminal court cases. Again, this abuse of their private social time is a problem not shared by men. Some men appear to take the view that women are 'sexually available' just because they are travelling alone to and from work. Indeed, women have discovered that they are not safe in their own homes, never mind on public transport.

Former Transport Secretary Cecil Parkinson launched a campaign on 9 November, 1989 to tackle muggers and rapists who 'imprison' women in their own homes after dark. Mr Parkinson told a press conference that he intended to make trains, London Tubes and buses safer for women and old people by spending millions of pounds on hi-tech safety equipment, and the recruitment of more guards on public transport (precisely the Government action called for by SOGAT print union leader Brenda Dean at the 1989 Women's TUC at Blackpool). Mr Parkinson also appealed to the public to be the 'eyes and ears' of his crusade by reporting crimes or suspicions to staff or the police. He pledged that the Government not only wanted to eradicate the crimes of mugging, rape, theft and hooliganism, he also wanted to remove the fear as well. Parkinson's proposed package was to provide better lighting and mirrors in dark passages, alarm buttons, closed-circuit television and new police radios which work underground. He said: 'War has been declared against the public transport thug. Whether it be on Tubes, trains or buses, the battle has begun. It is intolerable that people should feel prisoners in their own homes, unable to go out at night because they are afraid of using public transport. I find it astonishing and distressing to hear of people being attacked in full view of crowds of other travellers with no one lifting a finger to help.'

Mr Parkinson's statement came only two days after the *Daily Express* highlighted the plight of women who use public transport at night. Under the banner headline, 'Is Any Woman Safe Now?', the *Express* questioned just how safe any woman was after a judge freed a gang of youths who had terrorised a young nurse on the top of a bus, stripped her and mauled her while other passengers looked on. And it followed an *Express* report which showed that millions of women are terrified to venture out at night. Angry MPs demanded the judge's resignation after he had freed the three youths, part of a thirty-strong black gang, who had molested the girl. Judge Nicholas Medawar ruled out jail sentences on Wayne Richardson, eighteen, Leon Williams, sixteen, and Benjik Bahoum, seventeen. He told them: 'This sort of outrageous behaviour usually follows with a custodial sentence but I feel able to give you conditional discharges.'

The seventeen-year-old girl described the ordeal, which she said had changed her from a happy, outgoing girl into a nervous introvert. She told the *Daily Express*'s Kate Parkin: 'I want to tell my story because I wasn't allowed to speak in court. What happened was so horrendous. I feel that the people who did it laughed at me in court. I had my clothes ripped. I was touched externally and internally. All the judge did was to slap their wrists and tell them not to do it again. They accused me in court of wearing slaggish clothes. I had on a short white skirt above the knee and a white crossover top. I wasn't going to go out on Friday night wearing a sack.'

She told the *Today* newspaper: 'For him [the judge] it was just another day at work, but he has ruined my life. I feel like a laughing stock. I used to have coloured friends but I have lost them. I see them all just as blacks now.' The girl's father said: 'She is mentally and emotionally scarred for life. She was a bubbly girl but now she is always down. She will never lead a normal sexual life after this. She distrusts all men now, especially blacks. That's not racial, it's a normal human reaction. If they had been green she'd have disliked green people. One of the defence barristers implied she was asking for trouble because she was in disco clothes. But if she was stark naked no one had the right to touch her. Now she wears sackcloths and has gone to live away from it all in Scotland. They [the youths] should have been banged up for a long time. Now they'll think they can go around doing this sort of thing all the time. I'm staggered. My daughter was put through the worst ordeal imaginable. She said they were all over her like animals.'

His daughter had boarded a bus near Romford ice rink at 11 pm and had gone upstairs with a friend. Snaresbrook Crown Court heard how Richardson exposed himself and how Williams had climbed between the two girls. The friend fled but the victim was hemmed into her seat by the youths and molested.

Prosecutor Ann Cotcherg said: 'Brutally violated and panic-stricken, she broke free and, with her clothes in tatters escaped from the bus.' Her father added: 'She has lost all faith in British justice which she was brought up to treasure.' Said *Today* in its opinion column: 'Who can say they [the youths] were wrong to laugh when the judge in their case makes a mockery of justice? First Judge Medawar agrees to let the charges be reduced from indecent assault to insulting behaviour. Then he lets the three off with a conditional discharge. So they walk out of court with a smile on their faces while the wretched girl must bear a lifetime's hurt from their bestial attentions. Yet again a judge has taken a tolerant view of male assault on women. Other male predators will be encouraged, while women will have their worst fears inflamed. Male judges seem incapable of understanding the damage such incidents do to women. Cases like this should be heard by women judges. And certainly never again by Judge Medawar.'

FOUR

ATTITUDES TO WOMEN

It is often said that when men get together they talk about little else but football, beer and sex, and not necessarily in that order. Apart from the motor car and fishing bores, plus those fascinated by 'shop talk', most men find sex a riveting topic of conversation. It is a subject on which all men are self-confessed experts because, after all, there are usually no witnesses to testify to the contrary, apart from the partner in question. Men gloat and boast about their sexploits and adventures to anyone who is prepared to listen and some men frequently inflict details of their conquests upon female company. Sad to say, many men view women purely as sex objects, objects of desire and lust and even useful playthings. Some men clearly do not listen while women are talking and some 'chauvinist pigs' would never dream of asking a woman for her opinion, particularly on 'heavy subjects' including religion and politics. While this information will not come as any great surprise to many female readers, it is still important that women, particularly the young and vulnerable, should have confirmed just what goes on in the minds of many men. It might help them to deal with harassers for a start, the men who spring — or should I say slither — from the ranks of the 'gentlemen' described above.

Creatures of habit most men certainly are and most women brag that they have got the male sex totally summed up. Indeed many have, if some of the female experts who have helped me with this book are anything to go by.

But for those who are still in the learning process, a

few home truths about men will not go amiss. Men have fought over women, argued over women, murdered for women and have murdered their women. Men have died for women while some join the Foreign Legion to escape from or forget women; others have committed suicide because they cannot have a particular woman or because they have lost a woman to a rival. Such is the fascination women hold over men. The very sight of a female captivates the male from a very early age. A good friend of mine, who I will not identify to save him eternal embarrassment, is an only child and did not see a nude female until he was about eight years old. The historic sighting, which took place on a beach, shocked him, because he could not understand why the poor child was not bleeding to death. This is by no means an extreme example and most boys have a story to tell about their exploration in childhood or teenage years of the female anatomy. In Gateshead, Tyne and Wear, around 1947, they used to call it 'playing doctors and nurses'.

What a great pity it is that any levity surrounding sex, and sexual matters, cannot stay like that. When sex becomes an obsession, as it does for a minority, the problems are there for all to see. The problem is there in pornography, the photographed degradation of women available for anyone to buy in respectable high street magazine and book shops.

Legislation has so far not interfered with the porn merchants who are making a fast buck out of this form of exploitation. More subtly, women are displayed as sex objects on hoardings and in advertising. Beautiful women are, apparently, essential for the market-men desperate to sell their special brand of lager, motor cars or chocolate flake. One newspaper is now a legend for putting bare female flesh, instead of news, all over page 3, while model Viv Neves attained fame, if not fortune, by appearing nude in Fisons advertisements in *The Times* newspaper during the 1970s. Holiday brochures, sportswear and leisure centres cannot be adequately sold to the public, it would appear, without the decoration of a nude, or near-nude, female on the cover of the advert. Fashion pages are becoming more outrageous in their display of the naked, or near-naked, female torso. The clothes on the girls are rapidly becoming somewhat irrelevant to the photographs. While the models concerned are laughing all the way to the bank, do any of them care what effect this has on a minority of men, such as rapists, gropers and harassers? Again, are these exploited girls and their advisers doing other women any favours?

There is the type of man who cannot 'get enough', collects female conquests like the Red Indians used to collect scalps, and has a running total of victories to tell his mates. Quantity is important for such men, who play the 'numbers game' (men, for example, who have not had more than fifty women are regarded by these superstuds as a variety of virgin).

Those who cannot compete with quantity resort to boasting about 'quality'. Indeed, James Bond himself has never mastered the sexual ability of one Fleet Street reporter whose stories are unbeatable (and impossible to check) for glorious technicolour, stamina and technique. I know one man who claims he has bedded 147 women 'so far' and can remember the first name of every one. No detail is spared the eager or unwilling listener. He is the sort of man who must satisfy, or attempt to satisfy, every female lucky enough to be in his presence. This is the real harasser, romeo and philanderer, when lust and power over his target become more important than love or affection. He is the man who cannot live without it, the sort of man who figures in most of the industrial tribunals now making news.

When I asked a conference delegate why, when drunk, he kept trying to get every female delegate into bed he said: 'It is a challenge. You have got to try, haven't you? If I go home without it I have failed.'

To some young men lust is more important than love.

Most men invariably understand lust long before they experience love. Sex they experience after lust and before love. Any man who says otherwise is unusual, fortunate or both. Or simply a liar.

The fascination of the female form has made a good living for artists, writers, sculptors, poets, photographers and designers for centuries and no man should feel ashamed at casting an admiring glance in the direction of a beautiful woman. Indeed, admiration from a respectable distance should be the hallmark of a gentleman. What a tragedy it is when men, of whatever age, overstep the mark and make total charlies of themselves. Harassment, an expression of power over women, certainly appears to start young. And it is in the home where parents can do so much to educate their male offspring. All three of my sons have remarked that cooking and washing are 'women's work' while my father would never boil an egg if my mother was in the house. Such nonsense was eventually knocked out of my chauvinist offspring who now do their share of the washing up and housework.

The sort of man who cannot keep his hands to himself starts young as well. Many a teenage girl will tell how she was 'accidentally touched' in tender places by a spotty youth. This 'accident', of course, is retold to his eager mates behind the bicycle shed in great detail, with essential embellishments and nothing left to the imagination. This 'boys will be boys' syndrome is, I suspect, universal, stretching from Peckham to Peking. Most women, like my colleague Christine Garbutt, experience it and learn from it. The professional harasser, however, does not know when to stop, and improves his lamentable technique into adult years. From my own observation I would hazard a guess that one male in every hundred is a regular sex pest. That is a conservative estimate. Only women will know how wrong I am. Worldwide the total must be staggering, if my estimate of 250,000 British sex pests is correct.

Sex pest stories I have come across cover a variety of types of men. For instance, a woman industrial correspondent once told me that an Arab journalist had offered her £1,000 for sex or £10,000 to be his bride. She slapped his face. Another woman reporter told me that a trade union leader offered to give her a 'scoop' if she went to bed with him. She preferred to miss the story. Both cases illustrate the bizarre behaviour of some men in the company of women. In the first case the man was a tourist and, presumably, could not behave back home like he did that day in Oxford Street. Nor could he understand why my woman friend had rejected such a magnificent honour. She could have become one of his assets while his prestige at home, at finding a British bride, would have soared.

A friend of a northern neighbour remained unmarried until he was thirty because he did not know how to talk to women, let alone behave around them. He was disgusting, touching women at every opportunity, swearing and making lewd suggestions in a loud voice. At parties, often drunk, he terrorised women and was ejected from many pubs and clubs. But he was a 'character' among the lads, and remains so today.

A divorced woman secretary eventually got the measure of him and tamed him. He is now as good as gold and happily married with offspring. But along the way he left a trail of female misery. Fortunately, his wife never lets him out of her sight, which is a blessing for everybody.

Men like to tell jokes about sex, women, lesbians and gays, and almost without exception most of these jokes are not funny, as well as being in the poorest possible taste. The dirty joke brigade cannot help themselves either, and have polished the art from the school playground to the office canteen. A good, clean joke is worth hearing if only for its rarity value. Clean jokes are well received, probably because the recipients are happy to escape hearing the filth. Again, this is a conditioning process which starts in the school shed and the boys' toilets, leading eventually to the soccer dressing rooms, rugby club bars and even the dining-room of the local Liberal club. In this respect, certainly, men never grow up. The problem with the dirty joke is that it assists and exacerbates the process of denigrating women in the eyes of men. Men should have the courage to tell the dirty joke merchants to shut up, and say so loudly. Once a dirty joke teller is addressing a silent audience he never returns for an encore. This pathetic minority of individuals are frequently harassers as well. The two seem to go together like toast and jam.

Certain aspects of the female anatomy are the butt of most jokes, with 'bums' and 'tits' among the favourites. In the eyes of many men women come well and truly labelled. Birds, frogs, tarts, dollies, dears, loves, darlings, sweethearts, gorgeous and duckies are a selection of the descriptions we have all heard.

Married men in the older age brackets frequently refer to their spouses as 'the wife', 'the missus', 'her indoors', 'the little woman', 'the battle-axe' and other terms of endearment while, I have no doubt, most married women have expressions of their own for *him*. Occasionally I meet men who refer to their wives by their Christian names and this makes such a pleasant change that I thought I ought to mention it.

The late Max Miller, who earned a living as a comedian, achieved a degree of notoriety in the 1950s by being banned by the BBC. This, of course, guaranteed him immortality. For the dirty joke battalion, he was a god among men. Most men thought him hilarious, and many women are reported to have split their sides laughing at his risqué banter. Feminism was not fashionable in those days and, as some young women will tell you today, it is often better to laugh than appear prudish and unworldly. If women were offended they maintained a dignified and tactful silence.

Much of Miller's line of patter was innuendo, playing

skilfully on the dirty minds of the audience. His *double entendres* were a speciality, according to those who saw and heard him. My only recollection is seeing him on television dressed in a ludicrous floral costume. His act, of course, was toned down for the small screen and I very much doubt, at that age, whether I would have understood what he was talking about anyway. I credit my late father for not finding him funny, either.

Peter Nichols, writing in *The Listener* in February 1959, rekindled my memory. Miller would stare at a woman in the front row, show off his silk suit and say: 'Do you like it, gel? Nice, eh? Would you like a feel?' Or: 'Are you sitting on a feather, lady? I had to take myself well in hand. Oops, hear that.' Or: 'I'm filthy with money', then, with a wicked look, 'I'm filthy without it.' Nichols remembered, although he was only twelve, the hypocrisy of the audience. 'What transfixed me was not his act but his audience; those same men who deprecated smut, those same women who dreaded familiarity with the working class they had so recently quit, all rocking and jerking, enthralled and excited, tickled into ecstasy as though Max had done it to each of them with his nice, clean fingers.' Then there were the wife jokes: 'I gave her a violin to give her jaw a rest. Someone said: "What's wrong with her mouth?" I said: "It's worn out."'

Miller would tease his audience with a white book and blue book. He would ask them which 'poetry' book they preferred to hear him read out. Naturally, they opted for the blue book. Nichols's father frowned on Miller's act and believed he gave commercial travellers a 'bad name'. Said Nichols: 'He disapproved of Max. But it was another, lesser comic to whom Dad gave the slow handclap one night at "The Hippo", shouting: "Women and children present", and finally forcing the man to wind up his act and get off with a song.'

The BBC ban, which some people would today describe as censorship and prudery, sentenced Miller to ten years off the air. They delivered this Calvinistic judgement: 'The BBC wishes to make it clear that there is an absolute ban on the following: jokes about lavatories, effeminacy in men, honeymoon couples, chambermaids, fig-leaves, prostitution, lodgers, commercial travellers, ladies' underwear. In short, when in doubt, take out.'

Nowadays, says Nichols, Australian comedian Barry Humphries 'is the heir to Max's territory. He can offer Joan Bakewell coffee with: "You look like a girl who needs something hot inside her."'

Miller used to say that sex was fun and life was good and that we must not let the killjoys win. Too true. But Nichols was right when he said: 'Happy is the land that needs no heroes and sad is the world that needs Max Miller.'

Most men prove that there is a Max Miller in all of us, but, just like a bad cough, you can always try to get rid of it.

If this chapter appears, to male readers, to be too hard on men, then I make no apology. If men were used, degraded, vilified, abused, and exploited by women they would be the first to complain and would want something done about it.

And it would be interesting to see whether they appreciated the jokes.

FIVE

TWO WOMEN IN A MAN'S WORLD

Lynne Gunning has become an unwilling *cause célèbre* in the history of industrial relations, but her story paves the way for other women who want to make it in a 'man's world'. When she started out, in 1983, to become a firefighter, she was blissfully unaware that she would soon make headlines which had nothing to do whatsoever with firefighting.

Guardian readers, too, had no inkling of what was to come when they read this picture caption on 24 November, 1983: 'Fired with success ... three firewomen, Lynne Gunning, aged 22, Liz Hollingsworth, 18, and Julia Blanchard, 18, who have just completed their basic training at the London Fire Brigade's training centre in Southwark. There is only one other full-time woman firefighter in the country.'

Lynne's ambition was to be a firefighter, make a living wage, and be good at the job. Some would say these are normal aspirations for most young people setting out on a new career. Originally from Wearside, family circumstances had taken her to New Addington, Surrey, with her adoptive mother. She found work as a traffic warden in Croydon, but decided to 'take the plunge' and tackle a traditional male domain — the fire service. She had heard that the Greater London Council, as it then was, was trying to recruit young women into the fire service.

Friends said later that it was a challenge she could not resist, and that it was never her intention to prove to men that she was as good or even better than they were. She simply wanted to be a firefighter, and an efficient one.

She knew the dangers and physical risks, but did not anticipate that these risks would arise from within the fire station itself. She was appointed a firewoman on 11 July, 1983 and on 28 November commenced duties attached to the White Watch at Soho Fire Station, Shaftesbury Avenue, London. She later told the *Today* newspaper that on her first day two men grabbed her when she turned up for work. One held her, the other threatened to rape her. It was their way of letting her know that she had entered a man's world, a world where it was important to be tough, resilient and 'one of the boys'. She says that on 20 April, 1984 she was assaulted, beaten and falsely imprisoned by colleagues at Soho Fire Station.

Her statement of claim, before the Queen's Bench Division in the High Court of Justice, provided details of her ordeal. It read: 'Fireman (Patrick) Toyne, Fireman (Garry) Langford and other firemen tied the Plaintiff to an extension ladder and tied her wrists together with a neckerchief. The ladder was placed over a hydrant, which was turned on. After about ten minutes, Fireman (Len) Goodfellow urinated from a first floor balcony into a bucket held by Fireman Langford. Fireman Langford emptied the contents of the bucket over the Plaintiff. The ladder was moved to a different part of the yard and the Plaintiff was left there for a further fifteen minutes. Fireman Toyne then called to the Plaintiff that if she was not prepared to shout out: "I want to suck your cock and swallow it", he would pour a bucket of water over her head.

'Fireman Toyne then tipped three buckets of water over the Plaintiff.' She told the *Today* newspaper: 'I went into the locker room but the blokes dragged me out and tied me to a ladder. They stuck me over the hydrant for half an hour for a soaking, then Patrick Toyne, Len Goodfellow and Garry Langford told me they'd leave me there all day unless I said obscene things. I wouldn't, so

Goodfellow urinated in a bucket and Langford threw it over me. It was disgusting. The station officer (John Peen), who was meant to be in charge, said: "When we chucked water over you your nipples stood out like gherkins." What was the point of complaining if someone in charge thought it was funny?'

That, however, was just the start of weeks of bullying, by the three men in particular. They thrust pornographic magazines in her face and chatted about sex. Then they began physically humiliating her. She told *Today*: 'I was lifting weights when Goodfellow stood over me and pulled down his trousers. Only when a standby officer from another station called him off did he go away.' Her statement of claim said that on 28 April, 1984 Toyne and Langford again 'assaulted, beat and falsely imprisoned the Plaintiff. At about 1.40 pm Fireman Toyne picked up the Plaintiff by her waist and carried her to a balcony where Fireman Langford was masturbating with his trousers down. Fireman Toyne attempted to seat the Plaintiff on his knee, but she struggled free.

'The Plaintiff, while stationed at Soho Fire Station, was subjected to further acts of indecency, humiliation, and harassment.

'On every day after 6 April, 1984 when the Plaintiff was on watch at Soho Fire Station, she was drenched with water by having a fire hose directed up her leggings or the front of her clothing. On 30 April, 1984 Fireman Langford exposed himself in the presence of the Plaintiff and started to masturbate. He said to Fireman Toyne: "You get hold of her, put her down and I'll fuck her" or words to similar effect. Later on that day Fireman Langford touched Fireman Alvers on his private parts and told the Plaintiff in obscene terms to do the same. On 7 May, 1984 the Plaintiff was mounting an appliance at the scene of a fire in the Haymarket. As Fireman Langford was mounting the appliance he said to police officers who were present at the scene: "You can fuck her if you like, she's an easy lay" or words to similar effect. Later on that day Fireman Toyne took down his trousers and Fireman Langford said to the Plaintiff, "Give him a wank."'

Lynne told *Today*: 'I was dragged onto the balcony by Toyne and saw Langford was behaving obscenely with his trousers down. Toyne tried to make me sit on his knee but I kicked him in the groin. Once Langford shouted to Toyne to hold me down. He undid his trousers and from his face he meant business. I froze with fear. I couldn't even scream. Luckily some men from another station stopped it.'

Lynne explained later that the statement Langford made to the police officer was the 'final straw'. She said: 'That was it. I couldn't take it any more. It sounds trivial but it was a slander.' Although she was due to spend another six months at Soho she was transferred to Clapham.

She was reluctant to make a formal complaint, but headquarters insisted that she put it all in writing. Five members of her watch were suspended pending investigation. In September and October 1984 disciplinary proceedings started under the Fire Services Discipline Regulations. After her transfer to Clapham, she says she was ostracised by her new colleagues and subjected to abuse. Newspaper cuttings were pinned on her locker door or in the mess on about six occasions. Says her statement of claim: 'Those men declined to speak to the Plaintiff unless absolutely necessary for the purposes of duty and the Plaintiff was subjected to intermittent abuse of a sexual character. In November 1984 the Plaintiff received at her home a series of obscene telephone calls. After January 1985 the Plaintiff was ostracised by the majority of men on her watch. In February 1985 the Plaintiff was obliged to move her bed from the dormitory to her locker room. After March 1985 the Plaintiff was ostracised by virtually all the men of her watch and subjected to increased abuse. The Plaintiff is thereby unable to carry out duties as an operational firewoman and by reason of the effect of the said matters on her health, she was placed on light duties on 8 April, 1985.'

Lynne's claim stated that on 22 November, 1984 she was prescribed anti-depressant medication by her doctor and was certified unfit for work until 14 December, 1984. She was obliged to consult the community psychiatric nurse on three occasions between November 1984 and April 1985.

On 6 April, 1985 she was again prescribed anti-depressant treatment. Formerly of good health, her statement said she was reduced to depression, anxiety and sleeplessness. Because of the disciplinary hearing, Lynne was unable to comment on the case to her new colleagues who had 'sent her to Coventry'. To make matters worse, the men at Soho were denying everything. Comments were added to the offensive newspaper cuttings calling her a 'back-stabber' and one said: 'Remember team work not back-stabbing.' On another occasion a photocopy of a magazine picture advertising a film was displayed showing a woman about to stab a man in the back. Fire Brigade rank markings had been drawn on the man's clothing and a caption added to suggest that the film advertised was entitled *Ice Station Soho* with a caption added to the effect, 'You are about to see Lynne Gunning stab her leading fireman in the back as she takes revenge.' One man made animal noises when he passed her while others called her 'slag', 'slut', or 'grass'. Another said: 'I hope you are not in the job just to prove a point, you have really fucked this watch up.'

Her statement of claim said that, apart from the obvious innuendos, she found offensive the suggestion that she could not be trusted as a loyal colleague. She was even told not to remove the offensive material from her locker because 'this would make the men more determined to persist in such conduct'. Later, a senior fire officer removed the cuttings himself prior to a station visit by a superior officer.

Said her statement of claim: 'It was obvious from the

content of the cuttings that they were displayed as a form of reprisal against the Plaintiff for giving evidence at the hearings.' The court heard that, even when Lynne was put on light duties as a result of her medical treatment for depression, she was mocked. One fireman was heard to say: 'I have just taken an asprin, can I have a day off?' Lynne told *Today* that she eventually suffered from paranoia that everybody hated her. The medical officer said so much damage had been done that there was no point in her remaining in the fire service. She said: 'I felt so sad and bitter. What a bloody waste.'

Once the story had hit the press, the Greater London Council offered to pay her compensation of £1,000, but her lawyer, Andrew Dismore, decided to take the matter to the High Court. He also decided to sidestep the Equal Opportunities Commission, for reasons which will be explained later. The press treatment, as always, was interesting, ranging from straight, reliable reporting to downright trivialisation. 'Fireman Gave Girl a Hot Time', 'Sex Pranks Firegirl Sues' and 'Firegirl in Ordeal of Shame' were typical of the tabloids. *The Daily Telegraph*'s Gerald Bartlett said on 18 September, 1984 that seven London firemen had been charged with sexually harassing a firewoman during 'bizarre' induction ceremonies. He said the seven were hauled before a brigade court of inquiry, held in camera.

Bartlett continued: 'Senior London firemen say the induction ceremonies are "traditional" throughout the service. Male recruits, they say, have all been through them "and a lot more". The seven, who risked demotion and/or fines under the Fire Service Disciplinary Code were: Station Officer John Peen, who faced three charges, including two of neglect of duty; Sub Officer Stephen Short and Leading Fireman Glen Grandison, who were similarly charged; Firemen Patrick Toyne, Garry Langford, Leslie Hemsley and Leonard Goodfellow, who were all charged with disreputable conduct.' Bartlett said that senior brigade officers regarded women firefighters as a 'rare and valuable commodity' since only five had come forward to join 7,000 male colleagues, despite rigorous advertising.

He said: 'To a certain extent they tend to blame this on reports of the Soho induction ceremonies and are anxious to "lay the ghost" of intimidation and unpleasantness meted out to new firewomen. He said regulations for personnel were laid down in 1947 when only male recruits were envisaged — so men had to be at least 5 feet 6 inches tall, physically fit, with good eyesight and not less than a 36-inch chest with a 2-inch expansion.' In a separate report on the Lynne Gunning inquiry, Bartlett said that new firemen had been tied to ladders, hosed down and ordered to 'skip around outside their stations in baby-doll nightdresses'. London Fire Brigade's Chief Officer, Ronald Bullers, was said to be 'shocked, embarrassed and dismayed' as details of various induction ceremonies among his men were given by a succession of witnesses.

Mr Bullers chaired the secret court with his Assistant Chief Officer, Gerald Clarkson.

Station Officer John Peen, thirty-eight, was reduced to the ranks for neglect of duty. He at first pleaded not guilty but later changed his plea. Mr Bullers said: 'He is not fit to be in charge of men.' His punishment was confirmed by the GLC's Public Services and Fire Brigade's Committee. His salary, upon demotion, was cut from £11,493 to a fireman's basic £8,415. Leading Fireman Glen Grandison was fined £350 for neglect of duty. Firemen Patrick Toyne, Leonard Goodfellow and Leslie Hemsley were fined £325, £300 and £200 respectively for disreputable behaviour. The case against Sub Officer Stephen Short was dropped. *The Daily Telegraph* reported on 23 October, 1984: 'Former Station Officer Peen is still called "guv" by his men who regard him as a "sacrificial lamb" of a "kangaroo court" of inquiry determined to salve its public conscience. Friends and men formerly under his command say he has taken demotion as a "major and insurmountable setback". One man said: "John Peen is a broken man. He was ordered to plead guilty to keep his job and now the career he worked so hard for is in tatters."'

Peen was posted to the Brigade's C division at Shoreditch as a 'buggy' driver, delivering papers and equipment around the East End. Fireman Garry Langford, twenty-five, was sacked for disreputable behaviour but later reinstated on appeal. He was then fined £250. A colleague said after the dismissal: 'He is in the depths of depression.

'I am stunned he should be dropped this way after risking his life in a dozen different situations. These initiation ceremonies do vary from station to station. It's true ours may have been a little colourful, but we never did anything to Lynne Gunning we would not have done to any other recruit. She asked to be treated like a man and she was.'

The newspaper said that firemen throughout the service were preparing to ask the Fire Brigades' Union to start an immediate campaign to change and improve disciplinary procedures which allow men 'to have their careers ruined by a kangaroo court'. They felt that, unlike the court of inquiry, future courts should be open and conducted by an outside body, unconnected with the fire service. The GLC's Public Services and Fire Brigade's Committee, in reply to written questions, said it was told that recruitment and training of women had created difficulties which had not been anticipated.

These were thought to include women's inability to lift heavy equipment and the reluctance of firemen to rely upon them as part of a team. One fireman told *The Daily Telegraph*: 'They are not a success in any shape or form. They can't lift heavy people, ladders and things like that and when your life sometimes depends upon the strength and competence of your mate it's very bad news.'

A Labour councillor, Miss Jenni Fletcher, faced demands to resign from a women's committee after helping to reinstate Garry Langford. The Greater London Labour Party's Regional Women's Committee wrote to Ken Livingstone, then GLC leader, asking: 'Whilst such a man remains on the fire brigade service, how can women in London rest easy in the knowledge that he might be one who has to come into their home, even their bedroom, in the event of some emergency or other?' The GLC's Public Services and Fire Brigade's Committee upheld complaints that Langford was guilty of harassment. However, the Committee overruled the Chief Fire Officer and reinstated Langford with the £350 fine. The Committee was made up of four Labour and two Tory councillors. Miss Fletcher, one of the Labour voters, was Vice-Chair of the GLC's Women's Committee. The Committee demanded her resignation and called on Langford to leave the service.

John Carr, Chairman of the GLC's Staff Committee, described the decision to reinstate Langford as 'despicable and disgraceful'.

Miss Fletcher told the *Guardian*'s Aileen Ballantyne that she was not happy about taking the decision to reinstate him, but said that she had 'good grounds' for doing so. Ballantyne quoted an unnamed official of the Fire Brigades' Union as saying that there was no evidence to justify dismissal. He said: 'Every fireman in Britain believes there is no place in the fire service for a female.' He said that in matters of physique, physical capabilities and strength women were not suitable. Harriet Harman, Labour MP for Peckham, told the *Guardian* that laws against sexual harassment were 'worthless' if they could not guarantee the protection of women workers against this type of treatment by male colleagues.

The Daily Telegraph came up with another story that a 'secret deal' had been struck with the Home Office. The 'deal' promised the men that their jobs would be safe if they pleaded guilty to the charges. In March 1988 the GLC and the accused firemen agreed to a full liability settlement without admission. Total damages were

£27,100—£25,000 from the GLC. Messrs Peen, Langford, Toyne and Goodfellow paid the rest from their own pockets. Said Lynne: 'There was no way I could have put myself through all that again. I would have gone mad.' The settlement was a significant increase on the previous record of £8,000 and a fortune more than the derisory £1,000 originally offered by the GLC. Lynne added: 'I have not done all this for the money. I have done it because I was so angry that the authorities allowed this to happen. Women like me were experiments.

'What happened to me will never happen to any other woman in the fire service. It has changed my life. Others have been spared at my expense.'

The Fire Brigades' Union, led by left-winger Ken Cameron, did not side with the harassers, officially, although I suspect many FBU leaders were with the accused 'in spirit' if the sympathy towards John Peen is a good basis for judgement. Nevertheless, the history books show that her union gave Lynne Gunning every support, and the union's journal *Firefighter* later warned members it 'would not tolerate' the sexual harassment of women colleagues.

The journal said: 'The case proves that individuals who commit serious acts of indecency can be liable to pay compensation out of their own pockets. The union will not tolerate any of its members being harassed at work.' Mr Cameron told me later that the fire service was 'very much a male preserve, but that was no excuse for what happened'. He added: 'No firefighter, male or female, should have been subjected to that sort of treatment.'

The story had an unusual ending. I discovered, quite by chance, that John Peen had enjoyed meteoric promotion early in 1989. This 'broken man', reduced to the ranks five years before, was promoted four grades up the pay ladder to the rank of assistant divisional officer, with a £5,000-a-year pay rise. His salary was increased from £12,000 to £17,000 a year plus London weighting. He is now in charge of 1,300 firefighters in North London.

Mr Cameron described Peen's promotion as 'astounding and inexplicable'. He said: 'London fire chiefs have turned punishment into a major promotion.

'If employers really care about equal opportunities they should set an example by taking the subject seriously. I just cannot see what they are playing at by this ludicrous decision. Mr Peen did not take part in the harassment of that poor girl but in a little station of 15 people he would have known what was going on. It was his responsibility to protect those under his command.' Mr Cameron stated that he could not remember a more spectacular promotion in the history of the fire service.

Commander Joe Kennedy, in charge of the North East London division of the London fire service said: 'John Peen is as good as anybody in the service and better than most. I find it sad that the union should rake up what was a tragic saga in the history of the London fire service. John Peen served his punishment like a man and lost £10,000 in wages which is bigger than any fine imposed in any service. He carried the can. Had he not been demoted at the time he would have become a divisional officer by now, earning more than £20,000 a year. He had an impeccable career record prior to this case and he has conducted himself with dignity ever since. He was promoted in accordance with equal opportunities procedures agreed by the union and management and he won promotion on the strength of his record, ability and interview.'

Lynne Gunning is understood to have returned to her native Wearside to run a garage business.

The rule book of the Fire Brigades' Union contains the following clause under rule 26, covering internal union discipline. Under I(e): *Offences* it states: 'A member of the union commits a disciplinary offence if that member discriminates against or harasses another on the grounds of race, creed, sex or sexual orientation.'

The new rule was adopted at the FBU's annual conference at Bridlington, Yorks, in 1988.

*

To illustrate just how world-wide the problem of sexual harrassment in the workplace can be it is worth looking at the case of Sunday Sanchez, a Miami Beach patrolwoman who was determined to succeed in the police force. Unlike Lynne Gunning, who had to quit to save her health and sanity, Sunday Sanchez challenged 'the system' — and won.

Journalist Margaret Hall, writing in *Today*, told on 23 August, 1989 of an extraordinary case in America involving Miami Beach Patrolwoman Sunday Sanchez, an officer who had been subjected to mental abuse from her male colleagues for several years. Her story is remarkably similar to that of Lynne Gunning in key respects. Sunday had found herself in a macho environment among crude men who clearly resented her presence. Sunday, with the support of her husband, Tony, took the Police Department to court and won an historic victory. The case 'stunned America', reported Miss Hall. Sunday was determined not to let the harassers off the hook because she wanted to win the psychological battle as well as maintain her position of principle. The harassment could have cost her her life, because male officers who should have known better behaved like spoiled schoolboys at the end of term, faced with an inexperienced replacement teacher. Once, when she requested back-up assistance over the radio, the 'evil nonsense' began, reported Hall. 'Mock moans of ecstasy, heavy breathing and the smack of blown kisses drowned out her voice.'

Eventually her patience snapped, and she embarked on the legal road which put her on the front pages. She said: 'I always fought hard not to allow the strain to affect the way I did the job. But it had to. It got to the stage where I dreaded going to work. I'd go in to sign on for my shift and there would be another lewd poster, another crude message scrawled on the wall. Then there would be a roll call, with the verbal abuse and all the time some superior officer yelling and cursing me out. Things got so bad I had to go to the bathroom to have a good cry before going out to my car. It helped to get me calm before going out on patrol. I never let those guys see me in tears, but I bawled my eyes out in private because of what they were doing to me. I was on the verge of a nervous breakdown. That is how bad things had become.'

Hall reported that Sunday had graduated from the Police Academy in 1982 as top of her year. At twenty-one, she was extremely bright, extremely fit, pretty and anxious to fulfil her childhood dreams of becoming a police officer. The first day she pinned on her shining badge as a Miami Beach police officer was the proudest day of her life.

'But from day one,' said Hall, 'Sunday was subjected to horrendous non-stop sexual harassment and verbal abuse from fellow officers. During her working day she was referred to as 'broad', 'whore', and 'slut'. She was even reviled as being gay, a false accusation which persisted even after her marriage. The favourite trick perfected by colleagues was to leave vibrators, used condoms and pornographic photographs in her locker.

For Sunday, it was not an induction ceremony, it was continuous. Just like Lynne Gunning, she endured sexual baiting on notice boards, including doctored cartoons, posters and adverts. She said: 'It was tough enough having to cope with the problems of the street without having all the harassment back at the precinct. I hate to admit it but it began to affect the job I did.' Sunday, who admitted using the odd swear word, refused to become 'one of the boys' by using foul language constantly. 'I didn't want to become like some of the other women who talk like truck drivers. I wasn't going to talk like a garbage pail just to make life easier for myself. There were days when I just couldn't face any more. I'd call in sick. That's what they drove me to — feigning illness to escape the misery.'

Her character changed and her force valuation marks dropped alarmingly as her work suffered. The harassment intensified after she teased a group of men that she could beat them at racquet ball. One even challenged her to a boxing match and fifty officers actually turned up one evening to see the arranged bout. Sensibly, she made sure she was out on patrol and missed the fight. Her problems mounted when she took up weight training and body building to add a few pounds. After winning a gold medal in the police olympics she was pictured in her local paper in a bikini. The next day the photograph was pinned to the sergeant's lectern at roll-call. Emblazoned across it was, 'No tits — just a dick'. Said Hall: 'Things continued to go downhill.

'She suffered a series of rejections when applying for promotion or training opportunities and requests to join the Juvenile Offenders' Department were ignored. Applications to join the Detective Bureau went unprocessed and, in spite of an urgent need for Hispanic speakers on the force, her request to learn Spanish was quashed. Taunts and ridicule became even more vile, but nothing she did seemed to help. Complaints fell on deaf ears. She was told that "horseplay" was a traditional part of political life and she would have to learn to live with it.' Sunday told Hall: 'It got to the stage where I knew I had to make a decision. I had three choices. I could quit. I could let things carry on. Or I could fight and get them changed. I couldn't quit. I wouldn't allow myself to. Letting things stay as they were was not on. So I had to fight ... And that meant a lawsuit. I had tried every other approach and nothing had worked.'

Sunday's mother had alerted the Police Chief to the fact that officers were disrupting her radio transmissions and putting her life in danger. Said Sunday: 'She was so angry she wrote to him saying that if anything happened to me, she would hold him personally responsible.' After she filed her lawsuit Sunday was transferred to front desk duties, which is usually a civilian job. Again, just as with Lynne Gunning, her decision to complain brought further odium upon her head. Obscene phone calls at all hours of the day and night, with some officers even threatening her physically. She even started carrying her gun off duty.

Coincidentally, she was promoted to detective just before the trial began. 'But the court saw through that ruse,' said Sunday. 'The day of the verdict was the happiest day of my life. I bounced out of the court convinced it was all going to change. How naïve I was. It just got worse. Now most officers won't talk to me. They cut me dead. They get up and leave when I walk into a room. I went to a union meeting to try and get things back on an even keel and half the officers walked out. Even the police chief hasn't had the guts to ask to see me, shake my hand and say: "Right, Sunday, let's start again." They have ostracised me because I broke the police code of silence. I ignored the golden rule — never talk publicly about what has happened in the force. My colleagues have been numbed by the court's reaction. They didn't think for one moment I would win. Hopefully women joining the force from now on will be spared all the demeaning abuse I suffered. Meanwhile, my future with the Miami Beach police looks bleak.

'Once again I face each day with trepidation. I could quit, but I won't have anyone saying I wasn't strong enough to take it. On the streets things are different. I am getting fantastic support from the public.'

Amazingly, the affair exposed the married Mayor of Miami Beach, Alex Daoud, as a sex pest. Sunday said he took advantage of his official position to confront her at every opportunity, chatting her up in public and humiliating her. She subpoenaed him to give evidence at her trial and he got a taste of his own medicine as his sexual harassment was revealed. Said Sunday: 'He was constantly trying to date me. He just wouldn't take no for an answer.'

She got no help from her immediate boss, Police Chief Kenneth Glassman, in keeping the randy Mayor at bay. At the trial a damning memo, written by him two years earlier, was produced. In it he dismissed her harassment as 'harmless horseplay'. He wrote: 'The majority of police officers take the attitude that if you cannot handle joking among each other, you probably can't handle it when things get serious on the street.' At the trial he said he did not order an investigation into her treatment because it would have been impossible to catch the culprits. But the verdict clearly shook him. 'I guess we are going to have to impress on each one of our officers the importance of even-handed treatment,' he said.

Sunday said she knew what it must have been like in court for a rape victim. She told Margaret Hall: 'They put the woman on the stand and say if she hadn't been dressed that way it wouldn't have happened, totally ignoring that somebody did something to her. It was the same with me. They attacked me personally, my characteristics, my appearance. They tore me apart. They did everything but address the situation.'

Surprisingly, she was not helped by fellow women officers. Sandra Kusbit glanced through the pornographic evidence and said: 'It's a matter of ignoring it. It goes away. Working in this atmosphere you expect it. I think they are funny.'

If Sandra Kusbit was being totally honest in that witness box it proves what my colleague Christine Garbutt said earlier — that what is harassment to one woman is not necessarily harassment to another. But why anybody, let alone a police officer, should have to tolerate that kind of conduct defeats this writer. Male officers told the court that Sunday was overly aggressive, surly and unsociable. Lieutenant Rocco Deleo testified that the lawsuit had killed off the traditional atmosphere of joviality that the precinct was known for. He said: 'We have reached the point where everyone is walking on eggshells.' The Federal Court trial had only come about after the police department ignored a 'verdict' from America's Equal Opportunities Commission condemning Sunday's treatment. The EOC's ruling had given the department two options — either make a written undertaking to change its ways, or face court action. The department did nothing and eventually went to court confident that no jury would take her side. In the event police chiefs faced humiliation and shame.

The courageous policewoman had two strong men behind her. One was her husband, Tony, a local prison officer. He said: 'There were days when she would come home and tell me the latest sordid episode and I would just want to jump in my car and confront those guys, but I knew it was something she would have to handle herself.' The other was Miami lawyer Bernard Waksler, one of America's top civil rights lawyers. He was horrified by her experience and took the case at once. He even waived his normal £200 an hour fee.

Sunday won substantial undisclosed damages. Her 'victory', in the glare of world-wide publicity, was an example of how courage overcame the embarrassment and humiliation she must have endured.

But how many women in her situation are prepared to suffer that for a career in a 'man's world'?

SIX

SEX PESTS AND A ROGUES' GALLERY

Sexual harassers can be found everywhere — at home, on building sites, in schools and universities, on trains, in the office and even on planes. The male feeling of superiority, using his perceived dominance to get his own way, is a feature of *Homo sapiens* which women combat from the cradle to the grave. Sometimes men must analyse themselves and admit to themselves, if nobody else, that they can be pests.

Their behaviour, putting women under mental if not physical stress, is something they can modify if only they stop to think for a minute just what they are doing. A regular in my favourite pub, for example, is a normal man in a traditional city job. In the bar he is a nuisance, embarrassing barmaids at every opportunity, commenting on their legs, hair etc. in a way which makes my flesh creep. Goodness knows what it does to them. Precious little, if their pained expressions are anything to go by. He calls them 'darling', 'love', 'dear', 'gorgeous' and 'beautiful' at every opportunity and enjoys chatting up other men's wives whenever the chance presents itself. When a barmaid asks him what he wants he invariably says, 'You know what I want, darling.' Should they really have to put up with that for £3 an hour? One evening a woman darts player invited him to buy a raffle ticket and he offered to undo his fly buttons instead. She smiled before moving on. I notice he never behaves like that when his wife is present.

A journalist from a 'respectable' national daily, not a

saucy tabloid, consumed large quantities of beer one sunny afternoon in a bar in Jersey and obviously took a fancy to a barmaid wearing what could at best be described as an 'off-the-shoulder' dress. He offered her £5 to show him 'one tit', an offer which did not endear him to the manager or the barmaid in question. He was shown the door. This particular man is good at his job, admired by his boss, loved by his wife and family but, once at large with alcohol, he becomes a one-man sexual harassment commando unit. He has had his come-uppance on numerous occasions but he will never learn. I will always admire the tough young lady on the train from Euston who broke two of his fingers when he took a cigarette from her mouth and threw it out of the window. After all, she was in a smoking carriage and was perfectly entitled to kill herself with nicotine if she wanted to. I doubt whether he will ever repeat that particular exercise and he does not like to be reminded of the incident, describing her as a 'hard bitch'.

A former office colleague had a track record of trying to get every secretary into his bed and he earned himself a doubtful reputation among the women who had turned him down. One day, in my presence, he asked a young secretary if she would like to have a bath with him. She flushed with embarrassment and left the room. When I asked him what drove him to do this, particularly as he observed that many of the office secretaries were 'unattractive', he answered that it was 'a challenge'. He said: 'I will soon be in double figures for this particular building and I want to keep it going before I get too old and past it.'

Barmaids, too, were victims at lunchtime and early evening, as were female traffic wardens who gave him parking tickets. Hotel receptionists were also targets for the bedroom and he made sure they all knew his room number whether they wanted it or not. Switchboard operators were 'chatted up' mercilessly just in case they got bored with the job and wanted to visit his room for excitement. He described himself as such a wonderful lover that every woman who succumbed to his charms enjoyed the experience of a lifetime, an event so marvellous that sex with any other man but him would be a 'non event'. He used to tell me and other colleagues that 'tears of joy ran down their faces' whenever he made love to a woman. This was interesting, because one woman who admitted going to bed with him 'just to shut him up' described him as the worst lover she had ever had. He was a dreadful sex pest, and women who failed to fall for his devastating charm and wit first time around were always treated badly. Secretaries who snubbed him were ostracised permanently. He stopped talking to one woman altogether on the grounds that she was 'physically repulsive'. Her 'mistake' was to have given him the brush-off.

Such men take it badly when their over-sized egos take a knock.

I cannot be the first person to notice that men bear an uncanny resemblance to dogs when it comes to sexual behaviour.

Let me explain. Just like dogs, men jealously safeguard their 'patch' or territory in the same way a dog will guard its kennel or its master's house or back garden. Some men do not like it when women encroach on their territory and perform jobs just as competently as them. Secretaries and other women in subordinate roles are there to be harassed, in the pest's eyes, to prove to him he is the man with the power. The women on equal pay and equal status, however, can be harassed for a totally different reason, hence the canine comparison. Executive women frequently have a torrid time in traditional male preserves like journalism and we have already seen what happened to a woman firefighter and an American woman police officer. Modern offices are a natural stalking-ground for the sexual predator who dislikes his female manager or 'fancies' a nubile young secretary. I fear that, with more women joining the British workforce, statistics of harassment will worsen before they get better.

The Alfred Marks Bureau Ltd published a survey *Sex in the Office* in 1982. It said that sexual advances have existed in the workplace since the day that women were accepted into business. 'This is not to say that the odd flirtation or love affair is a bad thing as long as both partners enter into the relationship willingly', said the report, after defining harassment as 'unwelcome sexual advances, requests for sexual favours, and other verbal or physical conduct of a sexual nature' which could lead to an 'intimidating, hostile or offensive working environment'.

It continued: 'Until recently sexual advances made by other staff at work, especially superiors, were only whispered about and suffered privately by the victim, who would not dare to speak up out of embarrassment or fear of being disbelieved, but would sort out the problem for her/himself, often resulting in a job loss, sometimes voluntary, sometimes not. In the United States the days of hiding harassment problems behind a smile are over and many lawsuits are filed not only against individual offenders but also against companies for sanctioning the behaviour of the harasser. In the UK employers, employees, unions and official bodies as well as the media are beginning to wake up to sexual harassment and to treat the issue far more seriously. We were keen to assess the problems, experienced not only by employees but also by the employer.' In order to carry out this investigation into sexual harassment in the office, two separate confidential questionnaires were distributed in January 1982 through branches of the Alfred Marks Bureau.

'One was completed by management and the other by office staff, enabling the attitudes of each group to be assessed and fairly compared. The results were subsequently processed by computer. As we do not believe that the problems apply solely to women, both male and female respondents made up the sample.'

The survey covered 799 people, of whom 455 were junior staff and 344 were management. Of the staff 82 per cent were female and of management 65 per cent were female. Those interviewed included married, single, divorced, separated and widowed people aged over 25 and under 60.

The size of the companies varied from those employing up to 25 people and those employing more than 5,000. Respondents were asked to explain what actions they considered were definitely, possibly, or not harassment. The report pointed out that 'everyone has his own opinion' of what constituted harassment and at what stage a sexual advance starts to cause distress. Some people find it flattering to be eyed up and down or whistled at, while for others these advances are embarrassing and distressing. Obviously much depends on the degree of persistence.' The Bureau's researchers found, not surprisingly, that almost everybody agreed that 'forcible sexual aggression' was definitely sexual harassment. Of managers, 98 per cent thought so, against 94 per cent of staff. One boss thought such behaviour was 'possibly harassment'.

From then on opinions varied widely. Direct sexual proposition was definitely considered sexual harassment by 80 per cent of all staff and 82 per cent of management. Three employees thought it was not harassment while 20 per cent of managers thought it 'possibly was'. 'Pinching or grabbing' was defined as sexual harassment by 75 per cent of staff and 73 per cent of managers; 26 per cent of management thought it 'possible harassment' and 24 per cent of staff agreed with them; 1 per cent of employees and 1 per cent of management thought such behaviour 'not harassment'.

When it comes to 'touching or patting' 22 per cent of bosses deemed this activity 'sexual harassment' while 42 per cent of employees also thought so; 63 per cent of managers thought it 'possible' and 44 per cent of staff agreed with them; 13 per cent of managers and 12 per cent of staff said it definitely was not sexual harassment. These results seem to indicate that the lesser the crime the fewer deemed it harassment.

Only when the 'bad behaviour' became more respectable did the views start moving in the opposite direction. For instance, being asked out on dates despite refusing was regarded as definite harassment by only 33 per cent of management and 36 per cent of staff; 51 per cent of bosses thought it possible harassment and 43 per cent of staff agreed with them; 13 per cent of management thought it definitely was not harassment and 18 per cent of staff agreed.

Some categories of harassment were not regarded too seriously by the workers questioned. For instance, being 'eyed up and down' was considered harassment by a mere 2 per cent of bosses and 4 per cent of employees; 26 per cent of bosses, however, thought it possibly was while 29 per cent of staff agreed; 71 per cent of bosses said it definitely was not while 64 per cent of employees agreed with them.

Although the report found that, while 'being eyed up and down' was not generally thought of as sexual harassment by respondents, almost three quarters did find 'suggestive looks at parts of the body' possibly or definitely offensive. Regular sexual remarks or jokes were likely to upset 48 per cent of employees and would definitely upset a further 17 per cent. The 'kiss on the cheek' on meeting or parting was mutually accepted by more than half the management and employees as a welcome or farewell gesture, rather like 'two men shaking hands'. Female employees definitely did not like to be touched or patted by their colleagues as 42 per cent felt this was definite sexual harassment, compared with only 1 in 3 males who thought so.

A few respondents said they found 'girlie calendars' or magazines distasteful while one employee felt embarrassed when colleagues or superiors spoke out about their sexual activities. 'Spreading rumours about a colleague's sex life can be a form of harassment,' observed one employer and a number of respondents summed it up by saying that if any of these actions are considered unwelcome then they can all be classified as harassment.

Of the 210 employers who had received complaints, 61 per cent stated that all, or the majority, were genuine and serious accusations. Examples volunteered included 'senior manager touching typist; secretary propositioned by boss who wanted to sack her when she refused to comply; manager telling female that her promotion depended on her willingness to accept his sexual advances; direct sexual proposition of a female worker in front of a client; middle-aged manager reducing sensitive 16-year-old girl to tears by sexual remarks.'

Two receptionists, the first in the suburbs and the second in central London, had problems with harassers. 'I was in the office alone with my boss and he thought he would take advantage of his position — he half raped me'; 'A senior tried to become too friendly and because I did not respond he became very forceful and aggressive, using very bad language which made me feel insecure.' Two female managers said that their senior managers had made it quite obvious that if they wanted to be upgraded they would have to be 'nice' to him. Bribes included holidays, preferential treatment and company benefits.

The Bureau set out a table indicating what action was taken following incidents reported by victims and this showed that: 53 per cent of the victims changed jobs; in 30 per cent of cases the company took no action; no culprits were dismissed; in 5 per cent of cases either party was transferred.

Men's fears of women encroaching into their once sacred domains comes across, once again, in the Bureau's report: 'A frequent comment from employees (perhaps surprisingly both male and female) was that some men feel threatened by the presence of women in management and sexual harassment was a way of undermining them in an attempt to assert their own status.' The report concluded: 'The turning point when a joke, remark, kiss, pat or even a look becomes a "sexual advance" rather than "an everyday action", depends very much on the individual's views, the initiator's intentions and the overall circumstances.

'While some office staff will laugh off anything but extreme cases of sexual aggression, others class a suggestive look or a wink as direct harassment. It does not simply come down to tolerance levels, however. It is very clear from this research that persistence by an unwelcome admirer plays the largest part in making a person feel that he or she is being sexually harassed. Probably the saddest fact of all is that the solution for the majority has not changed over the years and leaving the harasser behind by resigning their job remains the only alternative.'

The report said, however, that 'things do seem to be moving in the right direction, towards the day when every worker is aware of an official procedure to follow and sexual harassment is not regarded as an occupational hazard.'

A female personnel executive working in the suburbs had the last word: 'At last someone has taken the lid off something that has been suppressed for years — now let's do something about it.'

Some driving instructors join the rogues' gallery. On 18 August, 1989 the *Daily Mirror* reported that: 'A randy driving instructor who molested a teenage pupil was jailed for six months yesterday. Chelmsford Crown Court heard that Tom Jones, thirty-eight, undid a button of Cathy Tomlinson's T-shirt every time she gave the wrong answer to a Highway Code question. And he unzipped her trousers an inch each time she mistook a road sign. After more mistakes he put his hand inside her knickers.

'Jones, of Tilbury, Essex, denied indecently assaulting seventeen-year-old Cathy. When arrested, Jones told police Cathy had invented the complaint because he had shouted at her for bad driving.'

This example is evidently not unusual. Vaughan Freeman, Motoring Correspondent of *Today* newspaper, wrote seven months prior to that case: 'Claims of sexual harassment by driving instructors have increased nearly 700 per cent in the past two years. Such cases now account for 20 per cent of complaints to the Driving Instructors' Association, compared with only 3 per cent in 1986. The Association's General Secretary, Peter Russell, called on victims to speak out after revealing the figures yesterday. He said it was difficult to keep tabs on sexual harassment because there were only 53 Department of Transport inspectors to police 32,000 licensed instructors. In addition, the Department would not take any action in cases which did not come before the courts. The British School of Motoring suggested two precautions women can take to protect themselves against sex pests: "They should go to a reputable motoring school and check that their cars carry stickers showing the instructors are licensed." A spokesman added: "While it is impossible to vet everyone the chances of problems with a reputable firm are greatly reduced."'

Sex pests on the telephone have become another modern hazard for women, reported Juliet Rieden in a giveaway magazine *Ms London*. She said that the extent of the problem of obscene callers is an unknown quantity 'as it is wholly dependent on people reporting the crime'. She continued: 'In many cases the caller is known to the victim and so the victim is reluctant to report it. Also, there is the age-old problem with women when reporting any form of sexual harassment — they feel they will not be believed.'

She repeated Gallup Poll findings that one in every ten women in Britain receives at least one obscene phone call a year. 'That is over 2,250,000 women, all victims of fear.'

Miss Rieden said that British Telecom had produced a special leaflet to help anyone who is a victim of obscene calls and more recently had set up a special task force to examine the problem. Jan Walsh, Manager of BT's Corporate Customer Relations, said: 'The most important thing is to coordinate our efforts with the police, victim support groups and women's groups. We need to bring all these people together to work on the problem.'

Power, and the abuse of it, reek through most, if not all, the cases of sexual harassment clogging up the courts and tribunals. Keith Bradford, Community Relations Officer for Oldham, resigned in March 1988 after a four-week inquiry into his alleged sexual harassment of staff. Five female employees had complained about his behaviour. Bradford, forty-two, told the inquiry that he had exposed himself because his manhood had been challenged and had said to two secretaries: 'You won't see better than that this side of Cairo.'

He admitted that he had planted obscene sex magazines in the girls' desks, typed a pornographic sex game into the office computer and slapped a teenage Asian girl on the bottom while she was using a photocopier. The girl told the inquiry she was too frightened to tell her parents because she might lose her job. All five office girls said Bradford had felt their legs and breasts. He also tried to discuss his erotic fantasies with the staff, not appreciating that some people would rather he kept them to himself. He said: 'I want to stress that I am quitting and have not been sacked.' But the inquiry panel concluded: 'We feel that Bradford has abused his position. Sexual harassment had clearly taken place on many occasions with all female members of staff. We believe that he has behaved in such a manner as to leave us with no hesitation in unanimously recommending that he be dismissed.'

Here again we have the man with authority over women, thinking that because he towers above them in status he can behave how he likes ... the slapping of the bottom when there are no witnesses ... the girl's fear that she may lose her job in an area of high unemployment ...

the conceit that women want to know all about his sexual fantasies ... the planting of the sex magazines to shock them.

And all this while he was supposed to be at work!

How the young women were supposed to do their jobs efficiently while he was carrying on like that goodness only knows. Thankfully, they and their employers came to the same conclusion and did something about it. It proves, yet again, that harassment does not go away if you try to ignore it. As Valeria Mainstone of WASH says: 'It gets worse.'

Author Elizabeth Wilson may have been right when she wrote, in *Violence Against Women* (London, Penguin, 1983) that harassment has little to do with sexual attraction. She said it may be that it is the response of a man who has been genuinely attracted to a colleague but who, when he finds his interest not reciprocated, then becomes unpleasant, either by trying to force himself on her sexually or by, for example, spreading rumours around the workplace about her sexual behaviour.

As we have seen in the last chapter, nothing angers a woman more than when a man falsely spreads wicked rumours about her sex life. This was the 'last straw' for firefighter Lynne Gunning. Why spurned men do this I will never know. They know it hurts because the woman in question cannot prove otherwise. It might gain the men concerned a pathetic ounce of revenge, but it is counterproductive and they stand no chance of ever winning the girl.

SEVEN

THE CASE OF TIM PRESTON

When he started sexually harassing women and teenage girls at work, Tim Preston could not have realised that one day he would be the inspiration for a book on the subject.

The Preston case is a classic story of harassment. He abused his power over women and young girls in a bid to seek sexual favours and prove his 'masculinity' in the eyes of workmates and fellow lager-drinkers down at the club where he played pool. Preston was a leerer, lecher and toucher who antagonised, frightened and infuriated many of the women unfortunate enough to come under his authority. Even outside working hours he was still at it, talking to women with innuendos and using language guaranteed to shock. Whether the women were young or middle-aged, slim or plump, blonde or dark, it did not matter to Tim Preston. They were fair game, in his eyes, for his particular brand of fun. His case, unfortunately, is being replayed all over the country and all over the world all of the time.

Preston, then thirty-eight, was Medical Records Officer at North Lonsdale Hospital, Barrow-in-Furness, a quiet town better known for warships than for scandal. His job gave him power and authority over women, a power which he cruelly misused. Unknown to him, in the Autumn of 1988, one woman colleague complained about his behaviour to her local union official, who in turn reported the matter to her regional officer.

Her action was to start a chain reaction resulting in Preston's dismissal, disgrace, and the disruption of many people's working lives. Preston was last heard of working as a roofer, still earning his living in Barrow. One of his victims has since moved with her family to another part of the country to ensure that their paths do not cross.

Preston stands historically branded as a sex pest. 'Mismanagement with sexual harassment a secondary issue' was the official reason given to me for his dismissal. However, there are thirty-nine women, including thirteen YTS trainees and a college lecturer, plus a senior union leader, who say that sexual harassment was the prime reason for his departure. Preston's personal charisma, or lack of it as the case may be, was drawn to my attention by a woman SOGAT print union official over lunch. Preston's reputation, it transpired, had travelled almost 300 miles on the trade union 'grapevine' from one union to another. The official told me that the lengthy list of Preston's victims were, mainly, members of the local government union NALGO.

Barry Howarth, NALGO's Northern Regional Officer, was more than helpful. He was presiding over a dossier of complaints against Preston which he described as 'horrendous'. No less than twenty-six female employees at the North Lonsdale Hospital, Barrow-in-Furness, and the parents of twenty-three YTS students from the local college of further education had lodged serious complaints against Preston. Howarth had adopted the case almost as a personal crusade.

When I started investigating the case early in 1989, Preston had already been dismissed and was expected to appeal. Barry Howarth had arranged for me to meet four of Preston's victims at a local health centre. Three turned up and they were all understandably nervous; they had never met a Fleet Street reporter before, they had only recently got to know their own regional union officer, and they were gathering to discuss embarrassing details of their encounters with a sex pest. However, their motivation was revenge and a desire to ensure that Preston was publicly branded a man who really ought not to have power over women. All three said they would go to court on their union's behalf and that of the *Daily Mirror*, if necessary. All were prepared to give sworn testimony.

They had all worked with Preston at the hospital, where he was employed by South Cumbria Health Authority. Surprisingly, for a salary as modest as £12,699, he was in charge of sixty people. Mr Howarth said that twenty-six women had come forward to give evidence to the union once the first complaint had been lodged. A woman lecturer from the nearby college of further education also arrived to tell me about Preston's behaviour with some of her students. She complained that Preston had also tried to 'chat' her up as well, inviting her to a weekend medical conference and pointing out how costs could be shared by the use of a double bedroom. Howarth was furious with the local health authority, which he said was guilty of a 'cover-up'.

He had made this accusation in the local press and happily repeated the accusation to me. The authority's General Manager and Press Officer, Richard Priestley, was not very forthcoming when I first rang him. It took at least three very lengthy phone calls before I extracted the information that sexual harassment was a factor behind the dismissal. Priestley refused to read out Preston's letter of dismissal and became angry when I requested a copy.

One of the three women I interviewed told me she had taken another job to get away from Preston and that she was having medical treatment as a result of her experiences. Depression was one illness brought about by the harassment she had suffered, and she had lost three stones in weight. She had returned to her former job since Preston's dismissal and was helping other victims to discuss their experiences.

Barry Howarth told me: 'It is one of the worst and most distressing cases we have ever had to deal with. One woman is having psychiatric treatment as a result of her experiences at the hands of this man and others broke down when they told me about him.'

Preston, who lived in the town, started work with the health authority in 1982 and complainants say he started misbehaving towards women staff soon afterwards. They say he made regular sexual innuendos; promised promotion if they slept with him; victimised them if they spurned his advances; made them work longer hours without pay and denied them their holiday dates if they rejected him.

The woman who left her job because of him claims he told her new employers that she was a thief and incompetent. The woman college lecturer said: 'Everybody at the hospital knew about it, but it took outside bodies to do something about it and bring it to light. You had only to walk into the hospital to feel the atmosphere of hate against him.' She added: 'He hates me because I have shopped him and because I have organised the girls' statements detailing what he was up to. He tried it on with me as well. He suggested we share a double bed in a double room at an annual medical conference on the grounds that it was cheaper than two single rooms. I told him that, although his mathematics may be sound, my husband would not approve of the idea. Preston never forgave me.'

The first woman, Mrs A, told me: 'At an office party he came over, grabbed me and tried to kiss me. I told him that his efforts were not appreciated. He then struck up a conversation about my holidays and suggested that if I cooperated with him I could have my holidays and keep my job. It was the first time I had heard that my job was under threat. He told me that if we came to an "arrangement" I could keep my holidays. I told him I would rather be on the dole than do what he was suggesting. When I told him to go away he said: "When you leave give me your telephone number."' She claimed that after starting work with the authority Preston started making 'rude and improper suggestions'.

The second victim, Mrs B, said: 'I was standing in a local pub with a group of friends when I felt somebody nip and pat my bottom. I turned round and saw that it was Tim Preston. He was as surprised to see me as I was to see him. He said: "I did not realise it was you." When I objected to what he had done he said: "You would not know a good time if it hit you in the face."'

Victim three, Mrs C, said: 'I finally quit the job I loved because I could stand Preston no longer. I am having psychiatric treatment as a result and have lost three stones in weight through worry.' She continued: 'I was at a Christmas party when Preston walked behind me and grabbed my left buttock so hard that it hurt. I jumped forward at the shock of it. I turned round and gave him a look of disgust. He gave me a smug look and did not appear at all ashamed. I told him that his behaviour was not appreciated, that I did not like it and that he was a rat. He replied: "Your problem is you are too much of a goody goody."' Mrs C said that several weeks later Preston patted her bottom as he opened the door in the office. She says that on another occasion he 'squeezed my bottom again. I could not be mistaken. It was not an accident. When I told him to stop it once and for all he repeated his jibe that I was a "goody goody" and that I was uncooperative.' After quitting for another job she says he 'sought to ruin my reputation, professional standing and future career by telling malicious lies about me. He told my new boss that I was a thief, incompetent and a bad timekeeper.'

This allegation was supported by her head of department. The women complained that Preston was a 'constant nuisance' to female staff, making lewd suggestions and boasting about his sexual prowess. Said Mrs A: 'He was obsessed with sex and wanted to go to bed with anything in a skirt. He would rub up against you, drape himself around you with his hand almost touching your breast and advised us what he thought we should be wearing. I eventually became a nervous wreck and cried when I got home. I had to stop my husband going round to punch him on the nose.'

The college lecturer said that Preston called a teenage YTS student to his office and made an improper suggestion. When she tried to flee from the office she discovered to her horror that the door was locked. Parents of two of the trainees agreed to let their daughters' statements be read out to me. Both said that Preston attempted to push his way into a telephone box at the hospital when they were trying to make a call. One of the sixteen-year-olds said: 'He asked us: "What colour knickers have you got on?" Later in the pub he grabbed hold of my bottom and said: "Take your boobs out." He then tried to pull me towards him.' She added: 'A few minutes later I heard him ask another trainee to take her knickers off.'

The girl said that on other days when they were together in the office he would 'get too close to me and lean on me. I became very frightened of him and did not want him near me.' The second girl, also sixteen at the time, repeated the details of the phone box incident. She says that when she came out of the phone box Preston put his arm around her shoulder and 'patted' her. She said she was 'glad to get away from the hospital and Tim Preston'. Barry Howarth added: 'Apart from sexually harassing them they said he downgraded anyone who refused to cooperate with him and many were forced to work longer hours without pay. We then put pressure on management to resort to their procedures and the disciplinary hearing was the result. I could not believe it when so many women started coming forward with their complaints.' Preston was not at home to callers for several weeks after the local newspaper blasted the story all over the front page. 'Sex Case Cover-Up Claim' was the headline in the *Barrow Evening Mail*. Preston stayed with friends in town for at least a fortnight while his wife, Karen, fielded calls from the press. On legal advice Preston stayed silent.

Preston's appeal against dismissal failed, and he later dropped his case at a tribunal alleging unfair dismissal.

One of the women said later that she would 'never go through with anything like this again' in spite of the fact that Preston had been brought to justice. Barry Howarth said: 'The trouble with sexual harassment is that too many men think it is a joke. They believe that only physical contact, such as assault, is harassment and nothing else counts. It is about time men realised what women have to go through when they are being badgered by innuendo and suggestion. Many careers have been ruined as a result of threats to sack them or deny them promotion.'

He added: 'It took a lot of courage for these women to talk to their union and your newspaper. But they realise that men like this will only be stopped if women have the courage to stand up and speak out. Relating personal details is embarrassing and most distressing for them and some just break down. It is also terrible for their husbands and families who know what they are suffering but frequently feel powerless to do anything about it.'

Mrs A said: 'We were made to feel like the villains at the hearing, not the victims. Preston's lawyer really put us through it, an interrogation which included the colour of our underclothes. But we needed to stick together at such a time and see it through. It is good therapy to discuss the problem and talk about what happened.'

Mrs B said: 'Preston just loved having power over women and their careers and was obsessed with sex. Going to work became an ordeal. When he looked at me I shuddered because I could almost read his mind. He is a podgy creep who thinks he is God's gift to women and should go to bed with them all. Turn him down and your life is a misery.' Mrs C said: 'Many a time when I got home I just cried my eyes out. He has given us all a hard time but I will continue to speak out against him if ever he attempts to defend himself.'

Barry Howarth added: 'Harassment, like racial and religious discrimination, is an evil which is hard to prove, but victims must come forward and tell their stories to management and unions. Nobody wants to stop harmless fun at work and at parties, but responsible adults must learn where to draw the line.'

Mrs X claimed constructive dismissal from the authority because of her treatment by Preston. (The author has deleted specific dates to protect her anonymity.) In her claim form to the tribunal she wrote: 'I started work with South Cumbria Health Authority in ... In 1985 I was sexually harassed by the Medical Records Officer, including unwanted physical contact on three occasions. After I had made it clear that his advances were unwelcome, he started to victimise me. This included refusing my annual leave; making unfounded complaints; questioning my ability; refusing study leave; refusing to change my work patterns.

'I decided that I could not take this behaviour any longer and commenced a teacher training course at Barrow Technical College in ... with a view to leaving the authority. I gained my certificate in ... and was subsequently invited by the college to apply for a full-time teaching post. I applied but received no response and the post was subsequently readvertised. I learned that the Medical Records Officer had both contacted the Head of Department in the college and made untrue statements about me, ie, that I was a thief and fiddled my expenses and that my work was of a poor standard. Furthermore he indicated that he would not take students from the college if I was successful in gaining the post. I was not considered for the post. I subsequently applied for a part-time teaching post (12 hours) and was successful in obtaining employment with Barrow Technical College.

'I agreed with my consultant and with the Unit General Manager that I would work my contracted four weeks' notice, but because of a two-week overlap of the college term time with the period of notice, I could operate a form of flexitime for the final two weeks which would allow me to commence teaching and fulfil my contract with the authority. On Friday, 23 September 1988, I was told that the Medical Records Officer had refused to allow me to work my notice as agreed and that I had two options — leave immediately, or work the notice without the agreed flexible terms which would mean I could not take up my new job with the college.' She added: 'I consider that the behaviour of the Medical Records Officer from 1985 forced me to resign from my employment.'

The authority contested her constructive dismissal claim and she reluctantly agreed to settle out of court for £650 'in full and final settlement'. The authority, however, did not accept 'any liability whatsoever' in relation to allegations of constructive dismissal.

Preston was officially informed of his dismissal in a letter from Richard Priestley on 28 December, 1988. Priestley wrote: 'The reasons for your dismissal are, that you have demonstrated a gross incapability in carrying out your duties and responsibilities as District Medical Records Officer.

'In this respect, I have found that there are a number of specific issues, evidenced at your disciplinary interviews, which in summary relate to inability, and an apparent lack of understanding on your part in relation to your duties and responsibilities, an acute breakdown of working relationships with your staff, an apparent abrogation of your responsibilities on a number of issues, and demonstrated lack of insight into the managerial function of your department.

'These issues, taken as a whole, are, I consider, totally unacceptable in terms of the management of the District Medical Records function. I consider that there has been a fundamental breakdown in the trust and confidence in your abilities to carry out the duties and responsibilities of your post, by consultant medical staff, by certain of your staff, the Unit General Manager and myself. In addition, I have taken into account the allegations made against you by present and former members of staff, and one YTS trainee, concerning sexual harassment. I reserve my judgement on the position in respect of allegations of sexual harassment by other YTS trainees.'

EIGHT

THOSE WHO ARE TRYING TO HELP

There are more pundits than actual experts when it comes to discussing harassment, and it is worth looking at views and positive actions of some British trade unions. In my admittedly biased view, our unions have achieved much praiseworthy work in this field. After a slow and edgy start, the trade union movement gradually entered the frame by suggesting ways of combatting the problem in the workplace, particularly as many of the harassers are members of the same union as the victims.

The impressive lead taken by some unions has been eroded, unfortunately, by the male chauvinistic attitude of some TUC leaders who dominate the union hierarchy. In the past twenty years I have known women subjected to appalling harassment by a minority of trade union leaders who regard females as a necessary and almost obligatory adjunct to their already inflated egos. In their own headquarters some have been known to behave like tin gods, reducing their female staff to tears. Behind the security of their headquarters' front door, they can be just as 'powerful' and intimidating to staff as a 'captain of industry' in the employers' CBI. I remember one trade union official, many years ago, who offered to give a female reporter a 'scoop' in return for sex. She refused.

These examples, however, in no way detract from my genuine praise for so many male officials, as well as female, who have worked so hard in the past decade to put harassment firmly on the trade union agenda.

Britain's second biggest union, the GMB, led by John

Edmonds, has produced an excellent pamphlet advising members how to tackle the problem. Mrs Pat Turner, National Equal Rights Officer, says that harassment is any unwanted sexual advance and 'is usually the way in which a man shows or tries to establish authority over a woman'. She says that the harasser is often the woman's superior and this can make her working life unpleasant and difficult. 'He may make direct or indirect threats about the woman's job or career prospects.'

She adds: 'Sexual harassment means being treated as a sex object rather than a worker. Women do not "ask for it", any more than they ask to be raped, beaten or assaulted in any other way.'

Mrs Turner says sexual harassment is not fun and is not harmless. It has serious effects on women's health, on their work and on their personal lives. Many women feel obliged to 'laugh it off' or pretend they don't mind for fear of being thought a prude or a trouble-maker, or being accused of having no sense of humour. Women who are victims of this suffer from tension, fear and stress, says Mrs Turner, which can affect their ability to do their jobs. She says: 'This happens particularly when women are working in jobs traditionally held by men such as building, HGV driving and engineering. Men often use sexual harassment to drive women out of 'their' jobs because they feel threatened when a woman shows that she is as good (or even better) at the job than they are. So sexual harassment can be a way of perpetuating workplace discrimination against women by restricting their choice of job.'

She stresses that sexual harassment is a work issue and a trade union issue and 'is not just an individual or personal matter to be left solely to the woman concerned'. She advises in the leaflet: 'Don't ignore it! It won't go away. Your silence may be taken to mean that you don't mind.'

Mrs Turner gives women this advice:

Make it clear to the harasser that his advances are not welcome.

Find out if any other women at your workplace have experienced the same thing. They may think (quite wrongly) it's their fault, and might be keeping quiet about it hoping it'll go away.

Keep a record of each time it happens including date, place, what was said or done, and any witnesses you have.

Go to your union representative and inform him/her of what is going on.

A group of you could take on the harasser, and tell him unless he stops it right away, you will take the matter further. He may well be frightened by being confronted by a group of angry women!

Make a record of compliments on your work and other achievements in your work. Harassers often use false accusations of poor work as an excuse for getting rid of an employee who does not comply with their sexual demands.

Don't feel guilty — sexual harassment is an expression of power. Harassers may accuse you of 'asking for it' by the way you dress, or behave, or talk. But women are harassed regardless of these and regardless of age.

If you see another woman being harassed, go up to her and let her know she has your support.

Whether it happens to you or a workmate, raise it at the branch meeting and insist that the matter gets taken up.

GMB has an Equal Rights Committee in each region. Make sure they are informed of each case by writing a letter through the branch. You can ask for help from the committee if your union representative is the harasser.

Pat Turner states in her advice to union representatives:

Be aware of the problems that members face in bringing up such an issue. We are all brainwashed into thinking that women are to blame when they are physically or verbally abused by men, and it is difficult to stop ourselves thinking this way. Support from an understanding union representative will help members to overcome this.

Reassure the woman. She may be worried about what will happen if the incident 'gets out'. Let her know that you are concerned, and that the union wants to help solve this kind of problem.

Start building a case against the harasser, by encouraging members to keep a record of incidents. Try to get witnesses. This may be difficult because most harassment takes place in private. Do a survey to find out how many other women are being subjected to this kind of harassment. Get your case together before you confront the employers.

Keep it confidential until you have the agreement of the woman to do otherwise.

Encourage management to take steps to educate employees about sexual harassment, and to issue statements that sexual harassment will not be tolerated.

They should also provide formal channels of complaint, which can be used to take up grievances about sexual harassment.

Remind employers that they are ultimately responsible for harassment in the workplace.

In the past, it has usually been the woman who has been forced either to leave her job or to be transferred to another department, while the harasser is left in his job. Get a clause put in your agreement with your employer that the harasser, not the woman, will be moved or dismissed. If the woman would prefer a transfer, make sure she gets another job of equal status and pay.

Bring the matter up on union training courses, to

discuss with other representatives the best ways of handling the situation.

Mrs Turner's union has drawn up a 'model clause' on the prevention of sexual harassment which it feels should be a priority in the next round of annual negotiations with employers. The clause could be along these lines: 'The union and the employer recognise that the problem of sexual harassment is one that threatens women's jobs, promotion and training opportunities, health and wellbeing. Both parties to this agreement are committed to ending such harassment.

'Such harassment is any unwanted sexual advance, e.g. unnecessary touching or patting, suggestive remarks or other verbal abuse, leering at a woman's body, suggestive invitations, demands for sexual favours, physical assault. Grievances under this clause will be handled with the utmost confidentiality, and no action will be taken without the consent of the woman concerned. In settling the grievance, every effort will be made to discipline or transfer the harasser, not the harassed woman. Women employees as well as safety representatives and shop stewards will be permitted paid time off to attend training courses on how to deal with sexual harassment.'

The National Union of Public Employees, whose members are mainly female, represents nurses and town hall workers with some of the lowest pay scales in Britain. Its officers have had more than their fair share of harassment cases resulting from men in superior positions imposing their desires on their subordinates.

NUPE's Women's Officer, Maureen O'Mara, told me: 'Women, and some men, have been putting up with sexual harassment at work for decades. Usually women have just to put up with it — "it" ranging from putting up with remarks about appearance, their own and others, through to actual assault. Others have to face dealing with "cartoons" depicting workmates in suggestive poses placed on notice-boards "just for a joke", plus cartoons featuring themselves placed on their desks.

'Women put up with it because they believe that this is just the way things are. Their experience has often been that neither management nor the union will actually label this behaviour as a problem that needs tackling, particularly when the "harasser" is a supervisor as is often the case. There have been some changes, however, over the past five years or so. At national level unions like NUPE, with three-quarters of its membership female, have labelled this nuisance in the workplace a problem. Some unions, largely through the pressure of women members, have put together policies which first of all denounce sexual harassment as unacceptable behaviour and guide the union in the workplace on dealing with it.

'But national polices are one thing, trying to stand by them at grassroots level is often another much more difficult process. Women who complain have been described as causing trouble unnecessarily, upsetting the atmosphere in the workplace.

'If it gets to the stage where a woman feels she has no option but to make a complaint about the conduct of a fellow worker or her supervisor this can often throw up several problems for the union, particularly when both parties involved are members of the same union and expect support. The lodging of a formal complaint usually comes after the woman concerned, with informal support from her union, has requested the harasser to change his behaviour, in other words when she is at the end of her tether.

'There is a strong view that unions should not represent harassers in any disciplinary hearing with management. This becomes even stronger when union objectives at national level include the duty to "combat sexism and racism". But on the other hand it is argued who is to deny representation to a union member who has faithfully paid his subs over the years? Some unions aim to set up internal panels of members to decide representation, not an ideal solution but the problem is a very sensitive one and unions approach it in that manner. Many problems of sexual harassment are resolved informally through the presence in the union branch of experienced lay officials who know their members and management well. This informal approach combined with education and training of active trade unionists on the unacceptability of sexual harassment as part of the union's general educational programme is the way forward. Dealing with sexual harassment is far from being the responsibility of the union alone.

'There must be a commitment from management to deal with it swiftly as well as a strong message to the workforce that this kind of behaviour is not on.'

According to the Labour Research Department, an independent organisation, other unions vigorously taking up the issues are the Banking, Insurance and Finance Union (BIFU), the white-collar union APEX (recently merged with the GMB), the town hall union NALGO, the Society of Civil and Public Servants (newly merged with the Civil Service Union), the National Union of Teachers (NUT), the transport union (TGWU), the Association of University Teachers (AUT) and the shopworkers' union USDAW.

USDAW's national policy statement provides for the running of training courses and taking up and publicising legal cases against harassers. In 1986, for example, it put in an industrial tribunal application against the Co-op garage in Bolton, following the harassment of member Gillian Hampson, although the company eventually settled out of court for £6,000. In another case the problem was resolved when USDAW members threatened industrial action. USDAW has also settled cases at the workplace. For example, after a grievance had been initiated against him, a supermarket manager was severely reprimanded and warned for swearing at an USDAW member in front of customers and constantly using sexually explicit language when referring or speaking to her. A store manager was later sacked when another USDAW member complained that he put his arm around her and kissed her after being instructed by the management not to touch staff.

Said a 'Bargaining Report' article published by the Labour Research Department: 'A particular problem facing unions over the last couple of years is how to deal with cases where the alleged harasser is a union member, rather than the "conventional case" of a superior harassing a subordinate.' Surveys have produced mixed results as to which is more common, but the LRD survey shows that a significant minority (18 per cent) of workplaces reported one or more instances of harassment by a person of a similar grade to the victim. A TGWU guide on sexual harassment described how the union dealt with such an issue: 'In 1981 two women members of the TGWU working in the canteen of an engineering company complained about the behaviour of the head chef, also a TGWU member. He was dismissed by the company for sexual harassment. The man approached the union for help, and the district officer agreed to attend the appeal hearing to check that the disciplinary procedure was properly applied. The sacking was upheld and the man asked the union to support a claim of unfair dismissal. The union advised him of his rights and how to make the tribunal application.

'The TGWU was not, however, prepared to fight the case because the evidence of sexual harassment was overwhelming and their women members in the canteen had wanted action taken against the harasser.'

In another case on South Tyneside NALGO had a problem when both victim and harasser were union members. In the end it was dealt with outside the formal procedure 'through an apology', explained the union representative, who added, however, that the victim 'was not satisfied'.

The most damning aspect of the LRD survey was that

the 'main harassers are managers', with the most common punishment being a warning. Failure to report incidents included fear for jobs, promotion, reprisals and the fact that the harasser was often the boss to whom incidents would be reported.

NALGO, the big local authority union, issued guidelines drawn up by its National Women's Rights Committee in a pamphlet entitled *Dealing With Sexual Harassment*. This union has been at the forefront of vital women's issues and can be rightly proud of its efforts in this particular field. NALGO also accepts that one of the major conflicts of interest for the union centres principally on the situation that can arise where both accuser and accused are NALGO members. 'We have to face these problems squarely, make the union's position clear and devise workable procedures if members experiencing harassment are to feel confident that the union can and will support them.' The fact that harassment stems from power, or the power men perceive themselves to have over women, is a theme taken up by the union, which sees unwelcome parallels with racism. 'The issues involved may be similar and neither can be viewed in isolation. These forms of harassment must be seen in the context of how black people and women are treated in society in general. Black women can, of course, suffer double discrimination. For them, sexual harassment is exacerbated by racism. Very often managers or men in authority are the harassers, and this can make reporting very difficult. There can be a huge gulf of experience between female junior staff and their bosses.

'Many of the discussions between women in NALGO on sexual harassment have highlighted the collusion that often occurs between male managers in making sexist assumptions about women staff.'

NALGO outlines in its explanatory leaflets why many women are afraid to report harassment — the prospect of not being believed, the fear of being ostracised or refused promotion, not to mention unwelcome publicity. 'Women often feel as ambivalent about reporting sexual harassment as they do about reporting rape. One of the major problems is that false accusation is felt to be as bad and damaging as the harassment or rape itself. This view can stop many women from seeking help. It is vital that we establish procedures that, while protecting the innocent, do not act as obstacles to redress for women who experience the stress and humiliation of harassment. NALGO's disciplinary procedure involves a panel of up to four people, appointed anew for each case from nominations received by the branch Executive Committee. The panel consists of at least two women and where the case involves a black member at least two black people. Where representation is provided for the harasser, the man's representative must not use tactics aimed at destroying the woman's character in order to discredit her claim.' Such tactics can include raising irrelevant issues such as her sexual behaviour, previous office relationships, her clothing and so on.

If the panel decides to offer representation it has to ensure that the level of representation given to the victim is no less than that offered to the harasser.

The guidelines accept that one of the major deterrents to reporting harassment is the fear of being involved in a public scandal. 'Workplace gossip and innuendo can be extremely distressing. Confidentiality in all dealings with the woman herself, management representatives or colleagues of the woman alleging harassment should always be paramount. In some circumstances the union representative may want to interview others to see whether they have experienced similar harassment but this should only be done with the consent of the "victim" and interviews should be conducted in private and without disclosing the identity of either party involved wherever possible. The interviewer should ask if they have suffered any particular type of problem, and if so by whom it was caused. All written communications from any branch representative to a management representative at any level or to branch officers or members should be clearly marked "confidential" (or other wording that guarantees it will arrive unopened on the recipient's desk). This confidentiality will hopefully avoid any embarrassment of the woman. It may also guard against allegations of libel.'

Unions are carefully selecting women to act as special advisers in these cases. Equality officers are an example. 'Many women feel reluctant to report sexual harassment to male shop stewards, and some branches have appointed women advisers or harassment officers to deal with such cases. Hopefully, in the long term there will be enough female stewards and branch officers to make this less essential, but in the meantime it is important that branches recognise the need to have a female officer available in certain circumstances.'

NALGO also advocates support for the victim: 'Harassment is always traumatic and in some cases women who have complained have been isolated by their colleagues or made to feel guilty. It is essential that the union provides support and assistance for victims in these cases and, as far as possible, alleviates the trauma involved in pursuing such cases.' The guidelines stress that the victim should not be moved to another job, unless she wants to be, or suspended by the employer or, alternatively, forced to continue working with the harasser.

Transport and General Worker's Union National Officer, Margaret Prosser, says in the TGWU handbook *Combating Sexual Harassment* that 'this degrading form of victimisation must be stamped out ... certainly the problem is not a new one, even if it has got a new name. If behaviour is sexual in nature, unwanted and adversely affects a woman's work, then that is sexual harassment.' She points out that it is not only attractively-dressed office workers who are harassed. 'It affects women in manual trades wearing protective clothing just as much.'

She continues: 'Although the number of publicised cases is still small, the incidence of sexual harassment is widespread. The embarrassment of relating the experiences and the fear of losing a much needed job can all too often lead to silence.'

Margaret Prosser agrees with the *Daily Mirror*'s Christine Garbutt that behaviour which may be offensive to one woman may not be offensive to another. But she says: 'The important distinction is that sexual behaviour becomes harassment when it is unwelcome and unwanted by the victim. No worker should have to tolerate or laugh off behaviour that they find offensive. The imposition of unwelcome attentions is very much a reflection of general attitudes towards women in our society. They help reinforce women's traditional role in society and in the labour force at a time when women are struggling for equal opportunities. A woman's livelihood may be affected if she feels she can no longer face a particular working environment. Women's jobs are important to them, to their families and to the economy. They have a right to work free from sexual harassment.'

Margaret Prosser calls on branches to examine and adapt current grievance and disciplinary procedures to deal with cases of harassment and says that this particular form of victimisation will only be stopped if men and women 'acknowledge its reality' and:

> Are prepared to talk frankly about the issues.
> Ensure that their own behaviour could not be construed as harassment.
> Are sympathetic and supportive to the victims and take appropriate action in their own workplaces and branches.

She offers the following suggestions to victims:

> Tell your union representative as soon as possible.

Keep notes of all incidents, and the date on which they happened.

Wherever possible get witnesses to provide factual material for the case.

Discuss with your representative and colleagues how best to resolve the matter.

The harasser should be asked to stop by you and/or your representative. If necessary this request should be put in writing and a copy kept, and warning given that the victim will consider pursuing her legal rights.

Margaret Prosser cites the case *Hyatt* v. *Smithko* of Salop Ltd, in which Mrs Hyatt won an unfair constructive dismissal case after she walked out. Her employer had pinched her bottom, tried to kiss her and made suggestive remarks. When she objected he told her how lucky she was to work in such a friendly atmosphere. That case was taken under the Employment Protection (Consolidation) Act, 1978 but, as Prosser says, the Sex Discrimination Act 1975 'goes further'.

She also recalls the 1977 case of *Western Excavating* v. *Sharp* in which Lord Justice Lawton said that 'persistent and unwanted amorous advances by an employer to a female employee would be conduct entitling her to resign and claim constructive dismissal'.

Michael Rubenstein, Chairman of the Industrial Law Society, Co-Editor of *Equal Opportunities Review* and Editor of *Industrial Relations Law Reports*, compiled a report for the European Commission in October 1987. After eighteen months of research his report, *The Dignity of Women at Work*, concluded that women who are sexually harassed at work have no adequate protection under the laws of any of the twelve Member States of the Community, including Britain.

He recommended an EEC Directive to prevent objectionable conduct recurring. Under existing laws, those who suffer harassment can at best hope for monetary compensation, he said. He suggested that sexual harassment should be defined as 'verbal or physical conduct of a sexual nature which the perpetrator knows, or should have known, was offensive to the victim.'

Mr Rubenstein said that there is no legal protection against sexual harassment 'despite mounting evidence that it seriously damages the working lives of tens of millions of women in the Common Market'.

He called for Community-wide legislation in the form of a Directive on the prevention of sexual harassment at work, which would have as its aim the protection of workers against the risk of sexual harassment by encouraging employers to ensure working environments free of sexual harassment.

His report recommended that any EEC legislation should formally recognise that sexual harassment is discrimination on grounds of sex, but he argued that this in itself would not provide an effective solution to the problem. Sex discrimination law is oriented towards providing compensation for those who have been discriminated against. This addresses the harm after it has been inflicted. He said what is needed is legislation which prevents the objectionable from occurring or recurring.

He said: 'Sexual harassment is a proven hazard with serious consequences for its victims.' Governments, he suggests, 'would not normally expect employees to work with hazardous substances or dangerous machinery with no recourse until they have contracted a disease or suffered an injury.

'They should not ask women to continue to work in an environment polluted by sexual harassment with no means of redress other than the possibility of compensation for the damage they suffer. Instead, they should take steps directed at protecting employees against the risk of sexual harassment.' He said this could best be achieved by an EEC Directive which would require each country to implement the contents of the Directive in its own law.

The proposed Directive, as well as defining sexual harassment as stated earlier, should place a legal duty on employers 'to take such steps as are reasonably practicable to establish and maintain a workplace free of the risk to employees of sexual harassment'. Employers would be legally liable for any unlawful harassment committed at the workplace unless they could show that such steps had been taken.

Where the employer was found guilty of permitting unlawful harassment, industrial tribunals should be empowered to require the employer to submit a plan for approval outlining the corrective and preventative action which the employer will take to ensure that similar acts will not recur. Such a plan should include an adequate procedure for dealing with complaints, training on how to prevent and deal with sexual harassment, and appropriate disciplinary measures for employees who contravene the bosses' policy.

Rubenstein accepts that sexual harassment is a new name describing an old problem and that generations of women have been subjected to unwanted sexual attention at work and outside the home. He said: 'The phenomenon came to be regarded as a suitable subject for discussion in the early seventies. The process began in North America, where it led to administrative regulations and judicial recognition that sexual harassment is unlawful sex discrimination.'

Awareness quickly spread to Western Europe, culminating in a series of resolutions from the European Parliament which recognised sexual harassment as a major problem affecting the 'dignity and rights of women' at work.

Sexual harassment, says Rubenstein, is imposed upon the victim, often by a superior in the employment hierarchy. The common theme is that it is verbal or physical conduct, sexual in nature or with a sexual dimension unwanted by the recipient. 'It is this characteristic which distinguishes harassment from friendly behaviour. It is not romantic behaviour, for it produces feelings of revulsion. It is not trivial conduct, for it can damage the victim's health and drive her to changing jobs.'

He said: 'It is not prudish or extremist to be against sexual harassment any more than it is prudish or extremist to oppose rape. Nor is sexual harassment at work an isolated phenomenon. Surveys in Belgium, Spain, Germany, the Netherlands and the UK all show that tens of millions of women in the EEC suffer sexual harassment in their working lives.'

Harassment, he says, is frequently a 'function of power' and, because women rarely have power over men at work, sexual harassment at work is mainly a problem affecting women, although men as well as women can be sexually harassed.

He continues: 'Because it imposes conditions of work upon women that are not inflicted upon men and deprives women of equal opportunities that are available to men without sexual requirements, sexual harassment fundamentally conflicts with the principle of equal treatment.

'Sexual harassment can have a devastating effect upon the health and safety of those affected by it. The anxiety and stress produced commonly lead to its victims being off work due to sickness, being less efficient at work, or leaving the job to seek work elsewhere. Sexual harassment, therefore, has a direct impact upon the profitability of the enterprise. From the standpoint of the women concerned, they suffer both the adverse consequences of the harassment itself and long-term damage to their career prospects if they are forced to change their jobs. Thus, sexual harassment is an obstacle to the proper integration of women into the labour market.'

Rubenstein points out that no Member State has any 'express legal prohibition' of sexual harassment and that, at best, it falls within the scope of the prohibition on discrimination in working conditions set out in Article

5(1) of the Equal Treatment Directive, because the gender of the victim is the determining factor in who is harassed and because sexual harassment at work disadvantages far more women than men.

He continues: 'However, only in the United Kingdom and Ireland is there relatively clear judicial acceptance that proven sexual harassment is unlawful sex discrimination.

'In other countries, use of equal treatment law as a remedy against harassment remains an academic hypothesis.'

Rubenstein, therefore, recommends that the Community should formally recognise that sexual harassment at work is discrimination on the grounds of sex for the purpose of equal treatment law. This should be done by means of a declaration stating that sexual harassment should be regarded as discrimination on grounds of sex contrary to Article 5(1) of the Equal Treatment Directive, and the laws of Member States should implement that Directive.

Rubenstein says that sexual harassment often takes the form of sexual blackmail, a distressing experience suffered by many women workers. He says: 'Sexual harassment at work should be unlawful either if it takes the form of "sexual blackmail" — where the victim's rejection of, or submission to, conduct of a sexual nature is used, or is threatened to be used, as a basis for a decision affecting her employment or her terms and conditions of employment — or where its consequences are such that the victim can reasonably complain that such conduct harmed her working environment. The latter concept provides a remedy for harassment which poisons the victim's working environment which is not conditional upon her leaving her employment or upon retaliation being taken against her.'

Rubenstein's research confirms, yet again, the perils women face when they seek justice. He highlights the extent to which legal complaints of sexual harassment appear to be deterred by rules of evidence which permit details of a victim's past sexual conduct and attitudes to be publicly disclosed, and by the prospect of widespread publicity being given to such evidence. He says: 'The act of sexual harassment itself constitutes an invasion of the victim's privacy. If, to secure redress, the victim must suffer a further intrusion into her private life in the form of public and publicised disclosure of her sexual attitudes and behaviour, few victims will wish to avail themselves of the opportunity.

'Therefore, it is recommended that a Directive should include a provision for the protection of dignity during judicial proceedings which would call upon Member States to take such measures as are appropriate to ensure that utilisation of the judicial process is not deterred by unwarranted publicity and does not entail an unwarranted intrusion into the private life of those pursuing their claims. Such measures might include holding judicial hearings on sexual harassment in private where appropriate; requiring the anonymity of litigants in sexual harassment cases to be preserved; ensuring that the rules of evidence exclude evidence as to a victim's sexual attitudes or behaviour with individuals other than the alleged perpetrator.'

Rubenstein says that, in order for a legal right to be effective, there should also be protection against victimisation for bringing a complaint to the employer or for instituting legal proceedings. He argues: 'This is especially important in cases of sexual harassment, because a common reaction to an allegation is to move the victim to another job rather than to move the harasser.'

The report concludes: 'Sexual harassment is not appropriate workplace behaviour. Few would seek to defend it as such. To be subjected to sexual harassment is an unacceptable working condition. Few would argue the contrary. Sexual harassment undermines the dignity of women and means that their working environment is less favourable than that of men. This is self-evident.

'And yet, in the Member States, there is no effective

legal means by which a woman can prevent sexual harassment at work from occurring and not much she can do when it has occurred. If harassment takes the form of a sexual assault, she can go to the police. But most harassment at work, albeit serious enough, does not rise to the level of a crime.

'If the victim is dismissed for rejecting an advance or for protesting, or if she resigns because work has become intolerable, she may be able to complain of unfair dismissal. But why should she have to lose her job to obtain justice?

'If she makes a complaint of sex discrimination, in a few Member States she may have a chance of success. But, at best, she will receive compensation for the loss which she can prove. The absence of legal complaints, when compared with the evidence from all over the Community demonstrating the high incidence of sexual harassment at work, makes it obvious that existing legislative provisions are inadequate. This cannot be acceptable.'

Rubenstein argues that a Directive on preventing sexual harassment at work will not cost money. 'Preventing it will save more money than the cost of permitting sexual harrassment to continue. A Directive would not represent an intrusion of the law into the private behaviour of employees. The distinction between relationships mutually entered into and the imposition of unwelcome and offensive conduct, once understood, is easily recognised.

'A Directive on sexual harassment would not conflict with equal treatment legislation. Sexual harassment is an obstacle which must be removed if the aspiration of equal treatment for men and women is to be realised. A generation ago, sexual harassment had no name. Without a name it was not regarded as a problem, and as it was not a problem, there were no solutions. Now sexual harassment has a name, it is recognised as a problem and the time has come for the problem to be solved.

'This generation of women has a right to expect that the laws of Member States will protect them against the risk of sexual harassment and allow them to pursue their working lives with dignity.'

Rubenstein concludes that the case for a Community initiative is 'overwhelming'.

More than three years later we are still waiting.

NINE

THE WORK OF DIANA LAMPLUGH

The chilling case of Suzy Lamplugh, the twenty-five-year-old estate agent who disappeared on Monday, 28 July, 1986, after showing a client around a house in Fulham, raised disturbing questions about the safety of women whose work requires them to be alone and unprotected. The anguish of the loss resulted in her mother, Diana, launching a tireless campaign, and the Suzy Lamplugh Trust, to promote the awareness of aggression in the workplace and to 'protect the many other vulnerable working women from suffering Suzy's fate'. She admits she could have shut the door to callers and pined away in her sadness, but Diana's resilience and dignity, amid a blaze of publicity which would have crushed so many, was amazing. She even overcame the trauma of a book, written by Andrew Stephen, suggesting that her daughter was promiscuous and neurotic and that her family relationships were frequently unhappy. In other words, Diana and her husband Paul were made to endure the age-old innuendo, promoted mainly by men, that their daughter was somehow to blame for her own disappearance.

The Lamplughs have been left to suffer the dreadful agony many parents feel when their loved ones disappear without trace, because, without a body to grieve over, their healing process cannot begin.

We may never know whether Suzy, an attractive girl who could be seen through the window of her office, was abducted or murdered by a calculating fiend.

Suzy was the archetypal daughter, a tennis-playing former chorister and girl guide, and very popular with both sexes. She was a former beautician on the *QE2* and a tireless partygoer, anxious, according to author Stephen, to move out of her own 'Putney set' and into the West End. The search for a solution has embraced many fantasies, including speculation that she is living abroad with the mystery 'Mr Kipper' or 'Kiper' whom the police have yet to trace. Diana Lamplugh is adamant, however, that Suzy would not have ignored so many family celebrations, including Diana's fiftieth birthday. Mrs Lamplugh told one journalist that she and her husband had 'known the full depths of despair and are now fated with her [Suzy's] character assassination and what I can only call our public crucifixion'.

Diana Lamplugh told Violet Johnstone of the *Sunday Telegraph* that she saw the Trust as her 'mission to protect working women from a similar fate to my daughter's. They must be aware of aggression at the workplace.' She has masterminded a 'relentless campaign', said Violet Johnstone. 'She has written books on self-protection for working women, lectured all over the country, and made a video package for schools.'

Diana Lamplugh has also laid the foundation for a national Missing Persons Bureau, run by the police and the Home Office, with an input from the Trust. She told Johnstone: 'It is far worse when there is no crime, because there is no end to the agony. It is seven years before a missing person can be declared dead, on paper. There are many people missing out there, and their families need advice on how to cope with the police and get the maximum publicity possible to help find them.'

Mrs Lamplugh joined me for lunch at the *Daily Mirror* on Thursday, 19 October, 1989, and confirmed what she had said to other journalists. The hurt and 'shock' of Andrew Stephen's book, however, would take time to leave her and her husband Paul. She said: 'We were shattered but we will get over it.' Her main anger was at the sheer irrelevance of Stephen's claims that Suzy was in any way promiscuous. Even if true, which Mrs Lamplugh denied, that was surely no reason why a girl should be abducted and murdered.

Mrs Lamplugh concedes, with reluctance, that Suzy is dead. She said: 'I knew the day she disappeared but you don't want to admit it to yourself, and I had to give a typical mum's support to the rest of my family. It would have been so easy to crack up, hide behind a closed door, and refuse to speak to the outside world. It was worse than a bereavement, because there is no body.'

The Lamplughs have no hatred towards Suzy's kidnapper, only anger. 'We would like her body to be found, so we can lay her to rest.'

Mrs Lamplugh has become an authority on sexual harassment since her daughter's disappearance. She said: 'I prefer to call it simply harassment because sex is not always the priority of the attacker, it is often the abuse of power. Boys and men suffer it from women bosses, although not to the extent women have to endure it.'

Journalist Anthea Hall, writing in *The Sunday Telegraph*, raised the sensitive issue of whether personal attractiveness, even sex appeal, should be a professional requirement in any job. She said this 'creates further risks, perhaps an invitation to danger. No sales force can be expected to prosper with either men or women who appear to dress at Oxfam, however much sartorial sloppiness might be a safeguard against unwelcome attention.

'The early vision of equal opportunity, which saw women as surgeons, pilots and business tycoons, paid perhaps less attention to the fact that the history of work has largely been a history of hardship and risks.'

Diana Lamplugh argues that men often feel a need to assert their authority over women colleagues with 'sexual power play' including commenting on a woman's attractiveness, and by addressing women with familiar endearments such as 'love' and 'dear' in front of male colleagues. She says in her book *Beating Aggression*

(London, Weidenfeld and Nicolson, 1988): 'A man might also use many words and gestures designed to undermine a woman's power and authority, and subtly diminish her in the eyes of other men. In order to gain power men may cast business relationships with women in the more familiar social male–female roles. The traditional male roles — father, husband, lover — are useful to men in the workplace because they help men to control women. Men will flirt with female subordinates, for example, in order to make it difficult for them to ask for rises or to refuse to do work that is outside their job description.'

Diana says that sexual harassment is 'debilitating, with stress-related illnesses'. She argues: 'How can anyone work efficiently if they are being sexually harassed?' She praises the work of WASH — Women Against Sexual Harassment — and welcomes the recognition by employers and trade unions that it is a problem which can be tackled by effective prevention mechanisms. She says: 'In many quarters sexual harassment is still seen as a joke. A large number of men are simply ignorant of the effects of their comments.

'They do not know what is offensive to women or why, nor do they understand that sexual harassment, even in its mildest form, can seem genuinely aggressive to a woman. However, we should remember that what one woman regards as offensive another may find harmless fun.

'The general rule is that conduct becomes unacceptable when the perpetrator knows, or ought reasonably to know, that it is unwelcome in the circumstances. It therefore follows that every woman should be fully aware of her own level of tolerance and have the confidence and support from her colleagues and employers to draw the line without causing offence or fearing recrimination.'

Diana Lamplugh believes that sexual harassment at work can be divided into six escalating categories:

Aesthetic appreciation: defined as appreciation of physical or sexual features. Remarks such as, 'I love that outfit, it really shows your figure.'

Active mental groping: such as men undressing women with their eyes, looking down blouses etc.

Social touching: apparently within normal conventions but with a caressing hand on the shoulder rather than a friendly hand.

Foreplay harassment: this is when the touching is more openly sexual. Men who consistently brush up against women or who are 'experts' at finding loose hairs on women's clothing or who 'helpfully' tuck in a blouse.

Sexual abuse: this includes verbal abuse, sexual propositions, hugging, kissing, direct touching.

Sexual intercourse: often the 'ultimate threat' when the victim is told her career prospects will be jeopardized if she does not consent to sexual relations.

Diana Lamplugh has analysed the type of men who are sexual predators and urges women to study their behaviour with a view to counteracting them. 'First,' she says, 'categorise the man.' Is he:

The older man who is just embarrassed by having women around the workplace, especially in authority. This man often makes the kind of comments which might pass for compliments in the social scene but are annoying in the workplace. This kind of colleague is best just accepted, as he is usually fairly harmless.

The likeable sexist who goes overboard when women are around. This man is likely to call you 'love' or 'dear'. Here you can employ assertiveness training [recommended in her book] and just remind him of your name. Repeat it again if he appears not to have heard.

The man who genuinely likes working with women and does not understand that his mild flirting is offensive. You might find it best to speak to him calmly and directly without rancour.

One of a group: Sexual humour is often used to create group feeling among men. It is usually directed at women to exclude them and give 'the boys' a sense of closeness with each other. Sometimes, however, it is hostile, aggressive humour directed against a woman and the woman's resistance is essential to the joke as it heightens the titillation. Avoid playing them at their own game. It is better just to ignore them and keep out of the way if at all possible.

If the situation continues have no hesitation. Go and discuss it with your personnel manager or trade union representative. Take a woman colleague with you if you find it easier.

A sexist pig or wolf: if a man is being truly obnoxious it will usually be obvious to others. You can ask them to help you if you find the man impossible to ignore. If he assaults you in any way, however, take action straightaway. I know that this sounds easier than it may be, for unfortunately the man in question could be your boss or manager or even a client whose account is essential to your firm. It is important to remember (and believe) that no man, whoever he is, has a 'right' to use you as a sexual object. It might be enough to discuss the situation with someone in authority and ask if you can be moved to another department or account. If this fails, talk to the personnel manager or your trade union. Consult **WASH** if you have no representative.

Diana Lamplugh says that women face harassment as part of their everyday lives, and that 'some factory girls have come to accept it as part of their life'. She told me: 'There are some odd but surprisingly upsetting incidences of sexual harassment which you usually have to face on your own. One which may seem trite, though it can strike you with particular force, is graffiti, which you may have to pass as you travel to and from work. I am not sure why it seems so personal. It might help to know that you are not alone.

'Streakers are usually seen as a joke. However, men with their backs turned, bent over and trousers down are a seriously aggressive signal in such countries as New Zealand. One of my friends had had a very unnerving experience. She works from home and had some workmen in to improve her office. After they left she took a film from her camera to be printed, and when she collected the photographs she at first doubted that they were hers — one of the workmen had taken a picture of his fellow builder in this position. The effect was distressing and abusive.

'If you have ever seen a flasher you will know that it can feel offensive. Pretending not to see an exhibitionist is the safest reaction. However, do try to look at his face and report him to the police. Flashers can progress to more violent sexual abuse and a profile at the station might come in useful when attempting to track a rapist.

'The calmest flasher I ever heard of was one who visited a woman I met when I gave a talk about the Trust. He was her plumber. She came into the kitchen to ask how he was getting on and there he lay under the sink displaying everything. She contemplated asking him to get up and leave immediately but then thought he might as well finish the plumbing first. Good plumbers are hard to find. Although she did nothing at the time, she did I am glad to say, report him to the police. I really admired her cool reaction, but I always wonder what I would have done in similar circumstances.'

A woman friend of mine had quick presence of mind when a flasher displayed his all on a tube train. Although petrified, she stared at his organ of generation and said contemptuously: 'Is that the best you can do? Put it away.' The man was humiliated and fled.

The Suzy Lamplugh Trust commissioned a report in March 1989, funded by Reed Employment, into *The Risks in Going to Work*. Written by Dr Celia Phillips, Dr Jan Stockdale, and L.M. Joeman, of the London School of Economics, the report covered 1,000 people — 800 women and 200 men. The survey covered sexual harassment, physical attack and threatening behaviour. The distressing conclusion was that, in the workplace, such behaviour is part of many people's working lives. The authors said: 'The workplace does offer a tractable arena for change but it will require greater awareness on the part of employers, unions and employees of the factors that contribute to such behaviour; policies and strategies for dealing with the problem, that take account of the specific circumstances encountered by different occupational groups; commitment and resources both to implement preventative measures and initiate training, which will translate policy into practical action.'

The report shows that the majority of sexual harassment cases occur in the respondent's own workplace, and that it is twice as likely to be perpetrated by colleagues compared with clients or customers. Not surprisingly, the survey found that such behaviour is 'primarily initiated by men towards women'.

It showed that, in just over a quarter (twenty-six per cent) of cases where no action was taken, the victims involved thought that their complaints would not be taken seriously. In a similar proportion of cases (twenty-four per cent) the victims were 'too stunned, surprised or embarrassed to do anything', and in ten per cent of cases they said harassment was the 'norm' at work. In another ten per cent of the cases nothing was done because of the seniority of the harasser, in a further ten per cent because the individuals wanted to avoid retribution from the harasser or from other colleagues, and in five per cent because they needed to 'keep the business or prove themselves in the company'.

In only a third of the incidents did the person harassed retaliate or confront the harasser, and in six per cent of cases the individual left or seriously considered leaving their job. In half the incidents described in the survey, those who had experienced sexual harassment had discussed it with colleagues or friends. However, only a quarter of the incidents were formally reported. The survey showed that men in superior positions are the worst culprits, making up thirty-six per cent of those guilty of harassment. The other offenders were a mixture of colleagues of equal status to the victim, junior colleagues, clients, customers and strangers. In 160 reported cases of harassment only six offenders were women.

Where did such incidents take place? A staggering seventy per cent, or 112 in total, happened at the victim's own workplace, with the remainder spread between other offices, shops etc., at the homes of clients or customers, in the victim's own home, over the telephone, at a hotel or conference, or while travelling.

Said the report: 'The picture that emerges of the nature of sexual harassment is of a mixture of isolated incidents and continuing behaviour, initiated predominantly by men towards women. Two-thirds of the reported incidents are harassment by colleagues, over thirty-six per cent of whom hold positions senior in status to the person being harassed. The majority of incidents fell into two categories. The first of these comprised sexual comments, innuendo and advances, which in some cases were accompanied by threats or offers of reward (forty-three per cent). The second involved physical contact, which in some cases was accompanied by comments and advances (forty-four per cent). Out of the seventy incidents involving physical contact, eight (eleven per cent) were categorised as assault, and included one case of sexual intercourse against the respondent's will. The remaining incidents included leering (three per cent) and the harasser removing their clothing (four per cent).

The report detailed the following comments from victims as typical examples of harassment:

> He would continually ask me how my sex life was, and who I was going out with. Would I like to go off one day for a walk, dinner, whatever. He was always leering and making remarks about my personal appearance and looks.

> I was told I would be promoted more quickly if I responded to his advances. I didn't do anything because I was embarrassed. I know I wasn't encouraging the possibility of anything but a working relationship.

> I didn't want to go to work, I avoided certain people at work and I asked for a transfer for 'career development'.

> Male clients at a building site leered, wolf whistled, and made cat calls, summoning their male colleagues, because of the rarity value of a female planner calling at the premises. The building industry is male oriented. I felt angry and annoyed, and reported it to a superior at work. He suggested I requested a male escort if I thought the behaviour might occur again. But you cannot predict when such incidents will occur, and it's impractical to request a male companion for site visits, in terms of both self-esteem and cost.

> A male colleague (superior) continually touched me, getting more and more intimate as time went on, finally culminating in indecent assault. I continually asked him to stop, and I reported it to my immediate boss. He thought I'd 'egged him on', but action was taken by another superior. It was entirely the harasser's fault. I was very angry. I was only 18, and people automatically thought it was my fault, being the office 'dolly' — it was awful and degrading.

I was continually harassed by a senior male colleague. On one occasion I was bending down to the bottom drawer and he bit my bottom. I hit out at him but he just laughed. It was common knowledge that this colleague harassed the girls, so it was accepted as the 'norm' by senior staff, and extra-marital affairs between upper management and staff were rife. I was very angry and embarrassed and I avoided certain people at work, as well as being bruised.

A senior male colleague introduced me to a group of male colleagues as 'having been laid on for their entertainment'.

When I was promoted above male colleagues, several of them accused a colleague on the appointments panel of rigging the promotion in return for sexual favours. This accusation was also made to my face in public. I did nothing. 'Making a fuss' would have been seen as weakness.

In a meeting I got angry about something that had been said, and I was about to walk out of the room, when a male colleague picked me up and sat me on his knee.

A male client continually makes suggestive remarks over the telephone, about getting together after office hours. I feel I can't do anything because he is a major client.

The report concluded that sexual harassment is experienced by one in five women in the professional groups as well as by those in retail and office jobs. For women in caring occupations, the figure affected is one in every twelve.

On 1 November, 1989, the *Independent* ran the following story: 'A 26-year-old woman flung herself from a moving car after being beaten and raped at knife point in the back of a bogus taxi. She had flagged down what she thought was a taxi on Monday night. It was the second attack in two days on women by bogus taxi drivers. When the driver began to take her to her home in Edgbaston, Birmingham, he turned up a secluded drive and attacked her. A police spokesman warned women to be careful when seeking taxis home.'

This news item appeared only days after Diana Lamplugh told me about the publication of a new booklet by the Suzy Lamplugh Trust entitled *Tips to Promote Safer Mini-Cabbing*.

John Quinn, writing in the *Mail on Sunday* on 29 October, 1989, said: 'Women passengers who have been attacked or raped by minicab drivers are to be asked to reveal their horrific experiences. They will be interviewed as part of a Government-backed research. Campaigners believe the results of the study will be so shocking they will finally force the Government to license all minicab drivers. Transport Minister Michael Portillo will announce tomorrow that the Government is prepared to fund part of the £40,000 which is needed by the Suzy Lamplugh Trust for the project. Already the trust has details of pornography being given to 10-year-olds by a minicab driver taking youngsters to school. And one young woman has written to the trust telling how she was badly injured when she jumped from a speeding minicab to avoid being raped.

'London's estimated 40,000 minicab drivers need only hold a driving licence. No authority checks on their background, the safety of their car or if they hold suitable insurance. Throughout the rest of the country any checks are at the discretion of local authorities.

'Labour MP Alice Mahon is to press Mr Portillo to ensure that the Government acts quickly when the results of the year-long research are published. She said: "At the moment we are asking passengers to put their lives in the hands of violent people." The Minicab Association, comprising the sixty largest minicab companies in London, and the Police Foundation are backing the research. Barry Irving, Director of the foundation, says the project needs more cash.'

The Suzy Lamplugh Trust's booklet of tips, compiled with the Metropolitan Police Crime Prevention Unit, says: 'Recent events have brought attention to the risks that can be faced, particularly by women, when travelling by minicab. To alleviate your fears and to help you avoid the rare but real dangers, here are some important tips:

Before you leave your home or place of work to go out for the evening, make sure you have with you the telephone number of a reputable mini-cab company. Just in case you miss the last bus, or a promised lift, you know that you will get home safely.

When you book your mini-cab, ask the company for the name of the driver whom they are sending. When he arrives to collect you, ask him to tell you his name and the name of his mini-cab company, to check that he really is the man sent for the job.

Get in the back of the mini-cab.

Try to share the cab with a friend — it's cheaper and safer.

Although it's natural to chat with your driver, don't give away any information about your personal habits — where you work, who you live with etc.

If your driver is taking an unusual route to your destination, or even travelling in the wrong direction, tactfully suggest a short cut to get you there.

If you feel very uncomfortable with your driver, ask him to stop and drop you off in a well-lit, busy place with which you are familiar, where you can go for safety.

If your destination is your home, ask the driver to drop you a couple of doors away from it — he doesn't need to know your exact address.

When you arrive at your destination, have cash

ready to pay the driver. Get out of the car as soon as you arrive, and then pay the driver through his window.

Have your front door keys ready in your pocket, and enter your home as quickly as possible.

Before you use any mini-cab company whose card or number you may have, check that they are the type of respectable firm which you are happy to use. Ask your friends if they know of them, check they're listed in the telephone directory or even go to see what their offices are like.

Think ahead about how you would protect yourself in the exceptional instance of harassment, robbery or assault.

If anything happens which makes you feel uncomfortable, get the driver's name and registration number and report it to his mini-cab company. Should the worst happen, go to the police.

Remember, most mini-cab drivers are reliable and honest. The last thing on their mind is trying to harm you, they simply want to provide you with a good service and a safe journey to your destination.

The Home Office issued an advice list to men, advising them how to help remove much of the fear suffered by women in everyday life. A three-year-old handbook, *Practical Ways to Crack Crime*, was updated to include key recommendations. Men are asked to keep their distance from women in dark streets at night, to keep away from them on buses and trains and not to give them 'admiring glances'. Says the booklet: 'Men can help by taking care not to frighten women and can make them feel safer. A woman may be nervous when she is out on her own, especially after dark and in a lonely or enclosed place, or on buses or trains.'

The advice lists says men should bear these points in mind in these situations:

*

If you are walking in the same direction as a woman on her own, don't walk behind her. This may worry her. Cross the road and walk on the other side. This may reassure her that you are not following her.

Don't sit too close to a woman on her own in a railway carriage.

If you are thinking of chatting to a woman waiting, for example, at a lonely bus stop, remember that she won't know you mean no harm.

Remember that a woman on her own may feel threatened by what you think are admiring looks.

You can help women friends or family members by giving them a lift or walking them home when you can. If you do, make sure she is safely indoors before you leave.

Don't enter a lift if there is a woman alone in it.

Remember that a woman alone could be your wife, girlfriend or mother.

The *Today* newspaper sought reaction from Tory MP Ann Widdecombe, who said: 'For the first time this shows men what responsibilities they have.' She added that men should be more protective towards women late at night. Alice Mahon, Labour, welcomed the new code, but accused ministers of using the charter to obscure 'their failure' to tackle the root causes of violence against women. Diana Lamplugh commented: 'We have to learn how we can behave, including how our body language affects other people.' Home Office Minister John Patten, launching the code, which was a £3 million phase in an £11½ million campaign, said: 'Women's safety is just as much a man's issue as a woman's issue.'

Mr Patten admitted that the Government had concentrated too much on property and not enough on the personal safety of individuals, particularly women. The campaign followed an eleven per cent rise in 1989 in the number of violent crimes.

TEN

FIGHTING BACK

Courage is often not enough when we are confronted by aggressors. Sometimes we all need a little help, and it is comforting to know that at least the law is on the side of victims of sexual harassment. The courage comes, of course, in knowing how and when to use it, or whether to use it at all. For the record, it is vital for women to know that sexual harassment is unlawful sex discrimination and is outlawed by the Sex Discrimination Act of 1975. This is because a manager or other worker who sexually harasses a female employee is treating her less favourably than he would treat a male.

A woman can complain to an industrial tribunal and seek compensation against her employer if her resistance to such harassment costs her her job, although most compensation payments appear to be poor return for the loss of a job or career. Employers should be aware that under Section 41 of the Sex Discrimination Act they are liable for any discriminatory act committed by their employees in the course of their employment. The defence to this is that the employers must show that they took 'reasonably practical' steps to prevent their employees from discriminating (ie harassing other employees). Women may also have claims for constructive dismissal where harassment forces them to leave their employment. In such cases they can argue that their employer's implied duty of trust and confidence in the employment relationship was broken when harassment was tolerated, encouraged or committed.

Employees should be aware that there is no minimum service qualification for protection against sex discrimination: workers are protected from sexual harassment from the very start of their employment and indeed before, if an offer of a job is conditional on sexual favours. There is no need to wait for a year or two before complaining.

Recent history has demonstrated, however, that legal statutory provisions are often inadequate to deal with a problem such as sexual harassment. This is where assistance is required in the form of practical help from friends, colleagues, neighbours, trade unions, sympathetic bosses, organisations such as WASH, the Women's Legal Defence Fund (discussed later in this chapter), or a damn good lawyer.

Jean Porcelli made history in a way she never intended or expected. In doing so, she paved the way for women to fight back. Like firefighter Lynne Gunning and countless others mentioned in this book, she fought the male-dominated 'system' and won. Her case was unusual in that the two men concerned were not seeking sexual favours. They harassed her because she was a member of the female sex and clearly resented her presence because she had entered their male domain.

Mrs Porcelli, then forty-five, was a laboratory technician at the Bellahouston Academy, Glasgow. She suffered such a campaign of deliberate cruelty from two male colleagues that she was forced to transfer to another school in November 1983. Backed by the Equal Opportunities Commission, she claimed that her case was actionable under the Sex Discrimination Act of 1975. She took her case to an industrial tribunal and lost, but won at an employment appeal tribunal. Her employers, Strathclyde Regional Council, the largest single employer in Scotland, appealed unsuccessfully against the EAT ruling at the Court of Session in Edinburgh.

The first tribunal had ruled that Mrs Porcelli, although subjected to unfavourable treatment, was not discriminated against because she was a woman. In their opinion, a man disliked by the two male laboratory technicians would have been treated in an equally unpleasant way.

The appeal tribunal, however, decided that the sexual harassment suffered by Mrs Porcelli was sex discrimination. The judgement, delivered by the Lord President of the Court of Session, Lord Emslie, together with Lord Grieve and Lord Brand, was memorable. Lord Emslie said that sexual harassment 'is a particularly degrading and unacceptable form of sex discrimination which it must have been the intention of Parliament to restrain'. Lord Brand stated that the men, Harry Coles and George Reid, 'pursued a policy of vindictive unpleasantness towards the applicant for the deliberate purpose of making her apply for a transfer from the school'. It was, he said, a form of unfavourable treatment to which a man would not be vulnerable.

Lord Grieve said the men had used 'a weapon, a sexual sword, unsheathed and used against the victim because she was a woman'.

The two men let heavy doors swing back on Mrs Porcelli when she was carrying laboratory equipment, deliberately failed to pass on information and instructions on the laboratory work, stored heavy apparatus and jars on a high shelf and swore at her when she was unable to reach them, and threw out her personal belongings. The men were said to have discussed pornographic films in front of her and on several occasions Mr Coles opened a tabloid newspaper at page three and commented on her physical appearance in comparison with that of the female nude depicted in the newspaper.

On another occasion he picked up a screw nail and, reported Mrs Porcelli, 'asked me if I would like a screw'. She said: 'Another example was when he picked up a glass rod holder, which is shaped like a penis, and asked me if I had any use for it.'

Both men claimed that she was 'lazy, told dirty jokes, used bad language' and was 'an unpleasant woman'. They also said she was prone to spreading malicious gossip about other staff members. Mr Coles denied all the allegations against him and said: 'I would describe her as not a very nice person to know because of some of the things she said to Mr Reid and myself which I thought were unbecoming of a woman. On several occasions she told dirty jokes and made suggestive remarks. I did not think it proper for a woman of her age to be using such language in front of blokes.' He claimed Mrs Porcelli spread stories about the personal lives of other staff members. Coles added: 'I wouldn't say I liked her as a person and as a working colleague I don't think she pulled her weight.'

A lawyer representing the employers said that the harassment was 'less disturbing at the applicant's age than it would have been for a young girl'.

Mrs Porcelli, who was awarded £3,000 compensation, said she felt 'totally vindicated' by the decision.

Incomes Data Services, in a briefing paper of December 1987, said Mrs Porcelli had been the victim of a 'policy of vindictive unpleasantness which included her tormentors making suggestive remarks and obliging her to brush against them in order to pass by. They aimed to force her to transfer to another school.' The IDS report said that 'embarrassing evidence is one factor that militates against women taking sexual harassment claims to a tribunal'. It added: 'It is an obvious criticism that a woman may be seriously deterred by the prospect of her personal life being under examination. Furthermore, it hardly needs stating that a woman's attitude to consensual or private sexual acts is irrelevant to the issue of unwanted, uninvited and specifically rejected sexual overtures.'

As a result of the case Strathclyde Regional Council drew up a series of guidelines to its 109,000 employees on sexual harassment at work.

Like Mrs Porcelli, Sally Muehring won a sexual harassment case although her superior was not after sexual favours. Unlike Mrs Porcelli, she managed to win out of court and accepted £25,000. *The Times* newspaper, reporting her case on 7 April, 1989, said she joined the publishing company EMAP in August 1987 to help set up a new financial magazine as its Director of Advertising and Marketing. In March the following year she had left the job, which she estimated offered a financial package of £50,000 a year, because of alleged sex discrimination. Rosemary Clunie reported that one year later she accepted £25,000 compensation for pain, suffering and loss of earnings, plus her legal costs, the second highest settlement of its kind ever awarded to a woman. Her lawyer, Denise Kingsmill, an expert on employment law, had filed at an industrial tribunal for sexual harassment and sued in the Hight Court for breach of contract, malicious falsehood, assault and battery, and aggravated damages.

Mrs Muehring, then thirty-one, accepted that her experience did not fit in with most people's understanding of the term 'sexual harassment'. She told Clunie: 'Sexual harassment is a very powerful label and much misunderstood. People think it's about sex, girls who get themselves into difficult situations. That had nothing to do with my case.'

She defined sexual harassment as 'really about power and using your gender to undermine your professional credibility and to diminish your authority', Her superior's decision to pat her bottom in front of sales staff 'was not a sexual gesture. It was about control, belittling me in front of my staff.' She finally walked out when she felt that, in a fit of rage, he was going to hit her. She contacted Denise Kingsmill and six weeks later legal proceedings started. An exchange of non-legal letters failed to reach an 'amicable' settlement over terms and the magazine made an 'insulting' offer while denying liability. An important part of her case was malicious falsehood, the alleged spreading of rumours after she left about her ability. The distress continued for months afterward, including lack of sleep and concentration and nervousness when meeting people. During negotiations, the company attempted to persuade her to accept a confidentiality clause. In other words, they wanted her to do a deal and keep silent. This she refused to do. She stuck to her guns and accepted the compensation offered, plus costs, five days before the case was due to be heard in court. The proposed confidentiality clause was dropped.

A spokesman for the company believed the denial of Mrs Muehring's superior. He told *The Times*: 'It seems very unlikely to me that anything happened. We couldn't prove it had not. There probably was quite a lot of shouting and anger. I think any man subject to that certainly would have put up with it. Maybe Sally was not able to put up with the stress.

'She had very good lawyers. We thought it would make more sense to pay the money and get rid of the problem.'

Mrs Muehring said the compensation did not make up for the loss of her job, but was significant enough to acknowledge that 'something happened which shouldn't have happened'.

EMAP and the executive concerned, who has since left the company, denied and still deny any liability.

Karen Harrison put the TUC women's conference firmly on the map one day in March 1988. When she approached the rostrum to propose a motion she could have had little idea of the furore she would cause. She was a twenty-seven-year-old British Rail train driver, a member of the drivers' union ASLEF, and a fighter for women's rights. Like firefighter Lynne Gunning, she had dared to find work in a traditional male domain. She had worked at British Rail for seven years and had become a train driver in 1985. When appointed, she was one of only two women drivers, together with one woman relief driver, and only about six women driver's assistants. As soon as her speech ended she was besieged by the media, and her 'ordeal by press' was to continue for the rest of the conference.

Her speech concerned the problems which women face in male-dominated industries and she delivered it straight from the hip, taking no prisoners. She spoke frankly to her trade union sisters about the appalling treatment she had suffered at the hands of her many male colleagues and revealed that a workmate had been sacked by British Rail for sexually assaulting her as she drove a train at fifty miles per hour.

The speech was a mini-sensation in Fleet Street terms. Because the Women's TUC is not considered newsworthy, few Fleet Street reporters were in attendance. But journalists were quickly mobilised by London-based news editors for the long journey to Blackpool to interview Ms Harrison. However, when they arrived they were in for a rude surprise. The lady was giving no interviews to anyone, apart from the only newspaper she trusted, the *Morning Star*.

As far as Karen was concerned, she had made her point and achieved the required publicity. Anything else desired by a hungry media was, in her view, typical scandal-mongering, sensation-seeking, gutter-press behaviour in a bid to ferret out salacious details of the assault. She could have been right although, as a senior Fleet Street journalist, I support the natural desires of editors and journalists to 'follow the story' and seek further interviews. I take the view that, once she had spoken to several hundred delegates at a public meeting Ms Harrison, unless she was totally cocooned from reality, must have realised that she was the centre of a news event. Her reasons for shunning publicity, however, must remain historically irrelevant. Her real achievement was to put sexual harassment on the agenda for the Trades Union Congress for all time. It was no longer an issue which could be ignored by the brothers in the movement.

Under the headline 'Victim of Male Abuse', the *Morning Star*'s Isolda McNeill reported: 'Woman train driver Karen Harrison yesterday listed an appalling catalogue of the harassment, isolation and degradation she experiences every day from her workmates.

'She told delegates to the TUC women's conference the "story of a woman train driver who started with British Rail in 1979 and after nine years on the footplate still has to contend with constant abuse".

'This woman's colleagues were "presently either sending her to Coventry or making vile jokes because she reported a colleague who was subsequently sacked,' Ms Harrison continued. "He was sacked for sexually assaulting her when she was driving a passenger train at 50 mph. This woman is me," Ms Harrison told a hushed conference.

'And she described how one day she was eating her sandwiches in the mess room when a colleague pushed a hard porn magazine close up to her face. Ms Harrison condemned "the serious under-representation and appalling treatment of women in male-dominated industries." She continued: "Such women come to conferences like this and are hailed as pioneers. But there is nothing as depressing, soul-destroying and lonely as being a flaming pioneer." She pleaded with conference to pass the ASLEF resolution which she moved on behalf of "women dying a thousand deaths every day they go to work." National Union of Railwaymen delegate Brian Arundel, backing the motion, declared: "I have seen it happen to West Indians, Pakistanis and women. Maybe homosexuals will be next."

'The successful resolution called for the targeting of traditionally male-dominated industries and the adoption of special measures both to increase women's representation and to support those women already employed in these industries.'

Helen Hague, the *Independent*'s then Labour Reporter, quoted Ms Harrison as saying that female trade unionists had covered up for their brothers for too long and that the movement needed a 'sharp elbow in the beer gut of male domination'. Hague said her speech 'highlighted the plight of women in male-dominated industries and encouraged unions to acknowledge the problem and exert pressure to end job segregation'. Maggy Meade-King, writing in the *Guardian* nine months later, quoted Karen Harrison as saying: 'There are a lot of nice people in the railways but it's the nasty ones, the big mouths, who make themselves known. I get a lot of abuse and there's really gynaecological pornography all over the walls, and yet, if I swear, the whole messroom descends into silence. But I like the job and I couldn't go back to nine to five in an office and I'm damned if I'm going to be driven out of my job by a load of ignorant people.'

A few days after her speech Karen again spoke to the *Morning Star*, which she described as 'the only paper I have any time for'. Because Ms Harrison still has no wish to be interviewed by a tabloid journalist, even for the purpose of this book, I am happy to quote freely from the *Morning Star*'s article — and my thanks to Isolda McNeill.

Karen said: 'The kind of men who harassed me daily have a big yellow streak. They never dared to say one insulting word to me when a union official was around. Union meetings are a different world, however. I have been elected Branch Vice Chair and I often chair the meetings but it's taken as completely natural by the activists. Unfortunately the men who show their resentment of a woman driver are not the type to ever attend union meetings.'

She said she had transferred to another depot for the sake of her physical and mental health. She said she had felt hostility from male colleagues from her very first day. Asked why she had persisted in a job which brought her so much daily heartache she replied: 'I love it. I would not say that I am an excellent driver, just average, but I love it.' Unlike many men, she passed her test at the first attempt. She continued: 'I have always liked trains and even when I was little and our family came to London from Glasgow where we lived, I always got my dad to take me round to the station. My job is a damn sight cleaner than nursing and it has better pay and better hours and conditions although our agreements are under constant threat from management. Before I joined the railway nine years ago I worked as a clerk in the Civil Service and I was bored. I wanted a satisfying job, and I have certainly got one.' Management, she claimed, was 'only barely tolerant' of women attempting to break into traditionally male industries.

She said she was convinced that the only way forward 'lies through trade union action. That is why I decided that I must speak out about the problems which I had been covering up for all this time.' She said a British Rail area manager had made sympathetic 'clucking noises' when she informed him in a two-page dossier of the incidents of sexual harassment which had led to her transfer request. 'He commented that he could not change attitudes and I knew that he was relieved that I was going.'

She added: 'It is crucial that lone women should not be isolated. I hear through my union activities whenever a new woman is going to start and I make a point of going to see her.' Her advice to women contemplating a career like hers is: 'I would advise them to definitely give it a go, it is a great job, and to join the union and get stuck in on both union issues and on making working life better for themselves and for other women.'

Karen Harrison and others like her may not thank me for saying this, but we all live in a male-dominated world. It follows, therefore, that men must hold the key when it comes to introducing change. After all, throughout the world men have overwhelming dominance in positions that really matter in society, such as politicians and judges. Men have more access to paid work because it is organised, mainly by men, on the assumption that male workers will have no domestic responsibilities restricting their availability.

Even when women can get paid work, they invariably discover that men are paid more. More men than women find their way into jobs with power and influence, while fewer men than women are channelled into what are considered lowly, servicing roles. The effects of sex stereotyping do not help. From their earliest schooldays, there are differences in the learning experiences of girls and boys. Girls learn to adopt caring and nurturing roles while boys are encouraged to take on more active and varied pursuits. Children are conditioned from birth to identify themselves primarily by their sex and, as tots, are given different toys.

Parents push their children into studies which are 'boys work or girls work'. Boys, for instance, are often encouraged to concentrate on science and woodwork, while girls are encouraged to concentrate on sociology or needlework. From the cradle to the grave many men are conditioned to believe that they are the superior sex in every way and consequently, most simply refuse to accept that harassment is an issue. To many, it is an ultra-Left-wing feminist distraction which we could all do without.

Here, I pay tribute to an article in *New Internationalist*, published in 1987, which must be the best 'dos and don'ts' charter yet aimed at men. Along with guidelines already laid down by unions and other organisations such as the National Council for Civil Liberties and the Equal Opportunities Commission, here are recommended actions which men can start taking — and stop taking — from today.

> Do ... listen to what women say. Men tend to dominate conversations and interrupt women's conversations as though they have a God-given right to hold the floor.
> Don't ... use pornography. Verbal and visual images stick in the mind and help condition male responses to women.

Do ... more housework. It is too easy to ignore the fact that toilets or ovens may need cleaning and that 'somebody else' will do it.

Don't ... be a physical threat to women. Avoiding women on a dark and lonely street by crossing over is a great help. Ask a man for assistance or the time rather than a woman, because women may be worried at your approach.

Don't ... indulge your awareness of women's bodies. Your attraction to the opposite sex may be natural but some men all too often have difficulty in being aware of anything else about a woman. Something to remember which might help is to fight your mental tendency to categorise women into separate physical compartments: breasts, legs, bottoms etc.

Do ... consider how your attitude to women at work could be considered an abuse of sexual power.

Firefighter Lynne Gunning won her struggle, quite simply, because her lawyers proved beyond doubt that her employers were in breach of common law. 'Implied' — a very important word — in her contract were terms that her employers would:

> Take reasonable care to ensure her health and safety.
> Provide proper and adequate supervision for their employees.
> Not expose her to foreseeable risk of harassment and ill-treatment.

There is a lesson here for all employers, trade unions, victims and harassers. The onus, clearly, is on employers to ensure that their workplace is a safe place, in every sense, for people to be.

Unfortunately, after all the courage she had shown, Lynne's nerve finally deserted her when the High Court case arrived. She settled out of court, although her legal advisers thought she would have won greater damages by giving evidence. But who can blame her for not wanting to relive the nightmare in the witness box? Bearing in mind that many women are too terrified to complain in the first place, Lynne's fight was an epic battle for justice. She had also endured the additional indignity of becoming a 'political football' used by Left and Right factions within the GLC to further their own aims.

Andrew Dismore, her solicitor at Robin Thompson and Partners, based at TUC headquarters in Great Russell Street, London, specialises in helping trades unions. Mr Dismore's company advises the Fire Brigades' Union, which brought the Lynne Gunning case to his attention. Mr Dismore said: 'The problem for any trade union in a case like this is that the harassed and the harassers are invariably in the same union. But you can only advise one party, and that has to be the victim. The men were represented by another firm and Mr Peen was represented by the Brigade. Lynne Gunning was a very personable young woman and a credible witness. She had clearly suffered a series of unpleasant experiences and had suffered physically and mentally. We decided to go to the High Court because industrial tribunals and the Equal Opportunities Commission do not result in high awards for the victims. We decided to go to the High Court, using common law as the basis for our case. It worked, although I still believe she could have done better if she had given evidence. By then, however, she had clearly suffered enough and she just wanted it all to end.

'There were hassles going on all the time, but she agreed to start afresh at Clapham Fire Station with a clean sheet. But she was ostracised there as well and treated as an informant who had grassed on her mates. Apart from the poor settlements reached at tribunals, there are scales of payments under the Criminal Injuries Compensation Board. But even with CICB cases the facts should be reported to the police. Also, the claimant has to explain why he or she did not go to the police.

'In the High Court there is no minimum payout and that is where the big money is. I wanted to see what extra cash I could get for her. After all, she had lost her job because of it and she was on equal pay. Firefighters are in the 'upper quartile' of male average earnings under a pay deal agreed with the Government after the 1978 firefighters' pay strike.

'You cannot get damages for hurt feelings, but you can prove financial loss and psychological injuries. Make no mistake, these blokes suffered very badly financially as a result of the case. Their bill must have been around £2,000 each, including compensation and legal expenses.'

Dismore added: 'When Lynne came to me there were no hysterics or tears or anything like that. She was simply brassed off with these men and wanted to do something about it, not only for herself, but for women firefighters who would be employed later. She was also upset that local politicians were trying to make political capital out of it. A generous ex gratia payment might have been acceptable at that time, early in 1984, but the GLC did not offer it. They offered only £1,000, which is little consolation for the loss of a career.'

The London Fire Brigade now has twenty-eight female firefighters and a code of practice for training women and ethnic minorities.

Brave pop star Linda Tolbert knew exactly what to do when passengers in a crowded London tube station ignored her cries for help when she was bothered by a sex pest. The S'Express singer tracked the man for an hour through London's busy streets. She refused to give in even when he hit her with a stick. Kate Parkin of the *Daily Express* took up the story on 18 October, 1989: 'She continued her two-mile chase until the pervert who exposed himself to her and a woman friend in Hyde Park was under arrest. The superfit American beauty, 26, known to her fans as Linda X, said later: "It was a truly terrifying experience, but I knew I couldn't give up. I was fighting for every woman who has suffered a sex ordeal."

'Yesterday as Mohammed Yusuf, 61, appeared in court for sentence after admitting indecent exposure, she was praised by police who said: "Linda was very brave, a real heroine." It was revealed that Yusuf, of King's Cross, London, was a persistent sex offender who had just been released after 11 years in Broadmoor high security hospital. Marylebone magistrates heard that Linda, currently high in the charts with her band's single "Mantra for a State of Mind", went to Hyde Park with a girl-friend one afternoon last month. Stewart Simpson, prosecuting, said they were pushing their bikes along when they became aware of Yusuf behind.

'They turned to see him exposing himself and screamed for the police as he walked straight towards them. She collared him after a lengthy chase by bike and foot, finishing with a fracas on a train as she dragged him off.

'Yusuf had a record stretching back 22 years for sexual offences in parks and tube trains. They included an incident where he forced a woman at knifepoint into having sex. Yusuf, released from Broadmoor in July 1989 after being committed for treatment in 1978 on an indecent assault charge, was remanded in custody for further psychiatric assessment.'

Madeleine Harper, writing in the *Mail on Sunday*, revealed on 22 October, 1989 how Linda, when seventeen, had seen her sex attacker acquitted. The memory of her experience had stayed with her, motivating her to 'arrest' Yusuf in such a dramatic fashion. Once again, her experience speaks volumes of the men — like the colleagues of Lynne Gunning — who failed to come to her aid. Said Harper: 'It was the memory of a nightmare that drove S'Express lead singer Linda Tolbert to pursue a sex pest relentlessly across London. For nearly an hour she tracked him, determined that he would not get away.

'Driving her on was the humiliation she suffered as a

17-year-old in America when she went through a sex ordeal. Like nearly every woman in the country, the former model has at some time experienced the unasked-for wolfwhistle and insulting remark.

'But last month, when a 61-year-old man exposed himself to her and a friend in Hyde Park, Linda Tolbert decided to fight back.' Linda told Harper that Yusuf had walked towards her and her friend and it was obvious what he was doing. She said: 'I shouted "Oh, you're disgusting" but he just carried on. Suddenly I flipped. I just didn't need this in a public park. If I wanted perversion I'd have gone to a porn show. I was furious.'

'Linda shouted at Anne-Marie (her friend) to get the police and sped off after the flasher on her bike. "If it had been dark, or if I hadn't had the bicycle, perhaps I wouldn't have done it," the singing star said, "but all I could think then was: 'This time I'm going to do something.'" The chase took Linda through a maze of back-streets as Yusuf tried to shake her off. "Every time he thought I'd gone he'd slow down and then he'd hear the wheels of my bike clicking round. It was like a nightmare for him." Eventually he fled into Queensway Underground station. Linda dumped her bicycle and ran down on to the platform, spotting her prey on a waiting train. She lunged towards him, grabbed him by the collar and yanked him off. While they struggled on the platform — the man punching at Linda and trying to break free — people just looked on blankly. "People were actually backing away from us," said Linda. "Even though I was screaming at the top of my voice for help."

'The exhausted Yusuf escaped back up to street-level, where two passing policemen finally arrested him. Linda clearly remembers the people who refused to help. The cab driver who lied that he was not allowed to call police on his radio. The man who said: "Oh, leave him alone, he only flashed at you." The fireman who told Linda that police were nearby but did nothing further to help. And countless others who did absolutely nothing. What makes

Linda's determination to bring Yusuf to justice so staggering is that she has already had bitter experience of the way in which the courts can treat females who allege they are victims of sex attacks. Linda says that when she was 17, she was attacked by a casual acquaintance in a friend's flat — a horrific experience she says she will never forget. But she remembers with even greater bitterness the court case that followed the man's arrest.

'She was subjected to an hour's cross-examination on her sexual history after which the alleged attacker, whom she barely knew, was acquitted of rape. Of her extraordinary chase, she says simply: "It was my duty. I cannot discount the occasions when I have been insulted by strangers who think they can get away with humiliating women." Men should think twice before they hassle Linda Tolbert — she is the kind of woman who fights back.'

Lawyer Denise Kingsmill, a friend of Diana Lamplugh, has seen her London-based firm inundated with claims for sexual harassment in recent years now that professional women, in particular, are taking their tormentors to court. Miss Kingsmill, like lawyer Andrew Dismore in the Lynne Gunning action, prefers High Court retribution rather than industrial tribunals where there is a statutory limit on damages. She said: 'We are seeing a significant increase in executive sexual harassment. Four years ago there weren't any sexual harassment cases being brought at all. Now we have around 50 a year.'

After the Sally Muehring case Miss Kingsmill's firm was asked to deal with thirty more cases. She added: 'One of the reasons is that women are working at comparatively senior levels doing competent and good jobs, but they are being harassed by men not as adequate as they are. It's a kind of macho aggressive management style.' Sally Muehring told Will Stewart of the *Daily Express*: 'It's nearly always a power-play, a senior male employee harassing a more junior employee. The rejected boss bullies her, gives her lousy jobs to do, diminishes or humiliates her in front of others, and makes working life intolerable. More often than not, she will leave before suing.'

Jo Richardson, Labour's Spokeswoman on Women's Rights, and MP for Barking, is delighted that, at last, women are standing up for themselves and taking positive action in the courts and elsewhere.

She tried and failed, in 1983, to push through a Private Members Bill aimed at merging the Sex Discrimination Act and the Equal Pay Act. She forecasts that, under a Labour Government, a new Ministry for Women will encompass all these issues, including sexual harassment. Miss Richardson told me: 'I am not trying to be wise after the event. I have been attacking sexual harassment in all its many forms for forty years and I am delighted to see that the problem is now being taken seriously. Women have lost job opportunities and their dignity in far too many cases. It has been an issue for most working women for most of their working lives and is not the factory joke it used to be. Thank goodness women are now speaking out and saying "enough is enough". Sexually-titillating calendars, unfortunately, are still with us and some journalists and certain tabloid newspapers do not help with their descriptions of women, but things are changing slowly for the better.'

She said that, under Labour, new laws will ensure that victims of harassment remain anonymous in court and tribunal cases. 'This will do so much to encourage more women to come forward.'

If sexual harassment is to remain an unspoken problem many women will continue to lose their jobs and suffer ill-health. Only by discussing the matter collectively can we all do something to right an age-old wrong. Certainly, nobody can legislate against attitudes, bigotries and prejudice, but society can legislate or act in defence of anybody who has suffered or is suffering as a result of those attitudes, bigotries and prejudices.

The use of the law, grievance procedures, tribunals, court action, direct action, union rule books and plain common sense can all be used to ward off the harasser, as we have seen throughout this book.

Lynne Gunning fought a tough, individual battle on behalf of all working women in a hostile male environment. She won the war but left her job. Karen Harrison won her war and stayed in her job. The women at Barrow-in-Furness struggled to free themselves from the mental scars of Tim Preston and at least one tells me she would never go through that ordeal again, even to secure justice.

All have one thing in common: when they were prepared to face the challenge they found an abundance of people ready and willing to help them.

The first step is to talk with other women at the workplace and discuss what to do about it. Collate all information and pass it on to your union representative or staff representative if your workplace is not 'unionised'.

Keep a diary or up-to-date records of the nature of the harassment, time and place. Women in the USA, in many ways the pioneers in this field, have even wired themselves for sound to gain evidence of the harassment. Tell the harasser to desist, and tell him in the presence of witnesses. If necessary, inform him in writing of the nature of your discontent and make sure you keep a copy. Many men simply do not realise what they have been doing or saying until it is spelled out to them. The touching, kissing and hugging brigade must be told that their actions are 'not on'.

Do not be afraid to create an atmosphere where sexual harassment, like smoking, is just not acceptable.

Employers, most of them men, should issue written policy statements setting out clearly that sexual harassment will not be tolerated and will be grounds for disciplinary action.

Supervisors should be encouraged to report specific

complaints and employees should report harassment to a specified management figure.

Early in April 1989, a Women's Legal Defence Fund (WLDF) was launched to help women who otherwise could not afford the advice and representation they need to take cases of sexual harassment to court. The Fund's founders claimed that all over the country victims of discrimination and harassment were being denied legal redress because they could not afford to bring a case to court themselves and were unable to find an organisation, such as the Equal Opportunities Commission or a trade union, to fight for them. Legal aid then provided only £75 in such cases to women on low incomes and that, too, only paid for advice, not representation.

Sandra Hempel, writing in *The Sunday Times* on 23 April, 1989, credited the idea for the fund to Maggie Monteith, a former officer with the Rights of Women, a research body. Said Hempel: 'She received an enthusiastic response from the lawyers she approached and has now set up a national network of lawyers and other experts to tackle cases of harassment and sexual discrimination. The service is free for women, and the lawyers are giving their time at no charge or at a low fee, which will be paid by the fund. The aim is to recruit enough volunteers so that the demand on the lawyers will not be great enough to deter them from coming forward. The fund will provide advice, help with preparing a case and representation at court or tribunal, and will also find a "best friend" to give moral and practical support throughout.'

Hempel reported that £70,000 had been raised for the fund's first year from such charitable organisations as the Nuffield Foundation and the London Borough Grants Scheme. The aim was to find £700,000 a year and to double the 200 lawyers and other expert volunteers within three years. Training courses were planned in advocacy, case preparation and listening skills, and seminars which would help lawyers to keep up-to-date with relevant legislation. She said the fund had a head office in London, where it hoped to have eight full-time staff, and was setting up ten regional offices, each with three staff, including a full-time lawyer.

The regional offices were particularly important, according to Monteith, the fund's Director. She said women were deterred because the Equal Opportunities Commission handled all its casework from Manchester. She claimed that another difficulty with the Commission, which welcomed the fund, was that it concentrated on cases which were likely to set legal precedents. Trade unions were also often unable to assist because many women are in poorly organised industries, while others are fighting cases about access to education or employment, which are outside union scope. Monteith said that, by filling the gaps in current provision, the fund hoped to make it possible for many more women to challenge the discrimination and harassment that affects their everyday lives.

Maggie Monteith says in the fund's promotional literature: 'Now is the time to say to women all over the UK that a practical way has been found to help them challenge the acts of discrimination faced by them in daily home and work life. Together we can provide a much needed service, to benefit all women. We mean to change the woman's world.' She says that, for over a decade, women have had legislation to combat many different forms of discrimination but, because of lack of know-how, financial support and expert backing, cases never reached industrial tribunals or were lost. The WLDF, she says, was set up to 'close gaps in present services, and to extend the pool of expert knowledge and skills in sex discrimination'.

The service is free at the point of provision and for women isolated and without support the fund's experts offer advice and information, case preparation, representation and 'best friend support'. Monteith adds: 'In short we want to change the world of work, education and services. By setting up the practical means, we aim to end sex discrimination.'

CONCLUSION

Alcoholism has been described as the 'forgotten disease'. If that is true then sexual harassment can surely be described as the newly-discovered forgotten problem, often overlooked by management and unions alike. To be more precise, ignored by men.

Women probably feel that, like cancer and the common cold, nobody will ever find a cure.

The easiest course, clearly, would be to disregard it, not write about it, never discuss it, and hope it 'goes away', like a headache. However, it is a problem which has finally been recognised and defined, not necessarily by men, but by women. Their judgement must be respected because they are the prime victims, have always been the victims, and probably always will be the victims.

Harassment is no fun, as these pages have shown, and can be a living hell for some. Lynne Gunning, Karen Harrison and Marnie Stinson are but three women among millions worldwide with such horror stories to tell. The only thing that sets them apart from other victims is that they have found the courage to speak out and say 'enough is enough'.

We have all met clones of Tim Preston and Mike Alway. They may have a different name and a different face, but they are still Tim Preston and Mike Alway. Men don't suffer from Tim Prestons. Of all the problems faced by working men — redundancies, sackings, demotions, muggings and other violence — sexual harassment is rarely one of them.

Men do not suffer from voyeurism, gropers, flashers,

sexual innuendos, sexual assault and the loss of promotion because they refuse to share the same bed as the boss. Men are unlikely to be ostracised because they turned down the golden opportunity of having an early evening drink with the supervisor or head of department.

Men are unlikely to be patted on the backside, have a hand pushed up their trouser leg, be praised for the colour of their suit, complimented on the texture of their hair or asked about the colour of their Y-fronts or boxer shorts. Nobody is likely to grab the cheeks of their posterior while they are bending over a filing cabinet.

Men will get home safely without being sexually attacked on tubes, buses, trains and taxis.

But I hope these pages have demonstrated that it is possible to fight back constructively, using common law, tribunals, the courts and codes of practice. Courage and common sense can play a big part and, yes, sometimes a verbal blast and a good kick on the shins can work in the right context.

Harassment is a social evil. Women should not be conditioned into accepting it as part of their everyday lives, as just another industrial hazard like metal fatigue. At least society tries to do something about industry's perils by appointing health, nuclear and railway inspectors.

But who polices harassment? We have seen how harassment leads to sickness, depression, absenteeism and the resignation of good workers. It is faced by millions of women every day on their way to work, while they are at work, and returning from work.

How I would like to ride into the sunset at this point saying that I have identified the problem, analysed it and that I have presented the perfect solutions. Unfortunately, I have not.

Sexual harassment is not heaven sent. It is *man*-made.

WHERE TO GET HELP AND OTHER READING

Sexually Harassed at Work?, WASH (Women Against Sexual Harassment), 242, Pentonville Road, London N1 9UN. Tel: 071-833-0222

Dealing With Sexual Harassment; *Working for Equality: a Summary of NUT Guidelines on Countering Sexism in Schools*, National Union of Teachers. Tel: 071-388-6191

Combatting Sexual Harassment, Transport and General Workers Union (TGWU), Smith Square, London W1. Tel: 071-828-7788

Sexual Harassment at Work, A. Sedley and M. Benn, National Council for Civil Liberties (NCCL), Rights of Women Unit 1982, 21, Tabard Street, London SE1 4LA. Tel: 071-403-3888

Women and Harassment at Work, N. Hadjifotion, Pluto Press

Sexual Harassment at Work: A TUC Guide and Workplace Programme for Trade Unionists, TUC, Congress House, Great Russell Street, London WC1B 3LS. Tel: 071-636-4030

Sexual Harassment at Work: IDS Brief 282/August 1984, Employment Law Briefing No. 69, Incomes Data Services Ltd, 140, Great Portland Street, London W1

Sexual Harassment is a Trade Union Issue, National and Local Government Officers Association (NALGO), 1, Mabledon Place, London WC1H 9AJ

Danger, Men at Work, Dr Rosalind Miles, Futura

Women's Legal Defence Fund, 29 Great James Street,

London WC1N 3ES. Tel: 071-831-6890

Women on the Move: Greater London Council Survey on Women and Transport, c/o Campaign to Improve London's Transport, 99, Midland Road, London NW1 2AH. Tel: 071-387-5019

Sexual Harassment Is No Laughing Matter, Equal Opportunities Commission for Northern Ireland, Chamber of Commerce House, 22, Great Victoria Street, Belfast BT2 2BA. Tel: 0232-242752

Sexual Harassment at Work, equal rights bulletin by GMB, Thorne House, Ruxley Ridge, Claygate, Esher, Surrey, KT10 OTL. Tel: 0372-62081

Code of Practice on Sexism, Association of Cinematograph, Television Trades and Technicians (ACTT). Tel: 071-437-8506

The Suzy Lamplugh Trust, 14, East Sheen Avenue, London SW14 8AS. Pamphlets include *Tips to Promote Safer Mini-Cabbing* and *Avoiding Danger: Aggression in the Workplace*. Tel: 081-392-1839

Sex Discrimination Decisions, Equal Opportunities Commission, Overseas House, Quay Street, Manchester M3 3HN. Tel: 061-833-9244

Women's Health Matters: Sexual Harassment, National Union of Public Employees (NUPE), Civic House, 20, Grand Depot Road, Woolwich, London, SE18 6SF. Tel: 081-854-2244

Code of Practice, Union of Construction, Allied Trades and Technicians (UCATT), 177, Abbeville Road, Clapham, London SW4 9RL. Tel: 071-622-2362

Are You a Victim of Sexual Harassment?, Civil and Public Services Association (CPSA), 215, Balham High Road, London SW17 7BN. Tel: 071-924-2727

The Risks of Going to Work, Dr. C.M. Phillips and Dr. J.E. Stockdale (joint first authors) and L.M. Joeman, London School of Economics and Political Science, commissioned by The Suzy Lamplugh Trust, funded by Reed Employment, March 1989

The Dignity of Women at Work, report on the problem

of sexual harassment in the member states of the European Communities by Michael Rubenstein, October 1987

Sex in the Office, an investigation into the incidence of sexual harassment, 1982, by Alfred Marks Bureau Ltd, Statistical Services Division, Adia House, PO Box 311, Borehamwood, Herts, WD6 1WD. Tel: 081-207-5000

Labour Research Department, briefing paper on sexual harassment, London. Tel: 071-928-3649

Index

academics' attitude to women in the classroom, 58
Accused, The (film), viewpoints concerning, 23–4, 29
Adams, Jane (of *Today* newspaper), talks to psychologist Glenn Wilson, 60
advertisements featuring the female form, 70–71
Alfred Marks Bureau, *Sex in the Office* survey, 97–101
Alway, Michael, case of, 49–55
APEX, positive action, 121
Arundel, Brian (of the NUR), supports Karen Harrison at TUC women's conference, 157
ASLEF, 155, 157; resolution pleaded for by Karen Harrison, 157
attitudes of men to women, 58, 69–76
AUT, positive action, 121

Bahoum, Benjik (molester), 67
Ballantyne, Aileen, interviews Councillor Jenni Fletcher on Soho Fire Station case, 85
Barclays Bank, employees' dress code, 28
barmaids as victims, 94–5

Barrow Evening Mail, reports Tim Preston case, 110
Bartlett, Gerald (of the *Daily Telegraph*), reports Lynne Gunning case, 82
BBC bans comedian Max Miller, 74–6
Beating Aggression (Diana Lamplugh), 137–8
Bellahouston Academy, Glasgow, case of Jean Porcelli, 151–3
Berrisford, Liz, case of, 38
BIFU (bank clerks' union), 28, 121
Birkhead, Vince, case of, 19–21
Blanchard, Julia (woman firefighter), 77
Blighton, Dawn, case of, 18–19
body language, 149
Bonner, Hilary, 26
Bradford, Keith (sex pest), 103
Brand, Lord, and the Jean Porcelli case, 152
British Rail, train-driver Karen Harrison's sex-harassment case, 155–9
British School of Motoring on sexual harassment by driving instructors, 102
British Telecom on telephone sex pests, 103

177

Brookside (TV programme), portrayal of sexual harassment in, 43–4
Brown, Owen (sex pest boss), 39–40
Bruce, Dr David (Senior Tutor, Corpus Christi), on academics' attitude to women in the classroom, 58
Bullers, Ronald (Chief Officer, London Fire Brigade) on the Lynne Gunning case, 83
Bush, Clive (CPSA Press Officer) at union conference, 8
Businesswomen's Travel Club on porn movies in hotels, 32
Butler, Lorraine (of the *Daily Mirror*), interviews victim of husband's rape, 37
Buxton, David (of Barclays Bank) on bank's dress code, 28
Byrne, Dorothy (ITV producer) on rape within marriage, 34, 35

Cambridge University, students suffering sexual harassment from dons and other students, 57, 58
Cameron, Ken (of Fire Brigades' Union), on Soho Fire Station case, 86
Capstick, Judge Brian, on rape within marriage, 36
Carr, John (GLC Staff Committee chairman) and the Soho Fire Station case, 85
categories of sexual harassment according to Diana Lamplugh, 138–9
Chaytor, Rod (of the *Daily Mirror*) on the Liz Berrisford case, 38
Civil and Public Services Association conference, incident at, 7–9

Clunie, Rosemary (reporter) on the Sally Muehring case, 154
Cochrane, Trisha (of the Businesswomen's Travel Club), on porn films in hotels, 32
Cohen, Barbara (lawyer), on rape within marriage, 36
Coles, Harry, involvement in Jean Porcelli case, 152–3
colleagues, support in sexual harassment cases, 46, 92
Combating Sexual Harassment (TGWU handbook), 125
Cook, Peter (Cambridge rapist), 24
Cotcherg, Ann, prosecutor in Kate Parkin case, 68
Crest Hotels, adult films shown in, 32–3
Criminal Law Revision Committee, 1984 ruling regarding rape within marriage, 34
Curtis, James, prosecutor in rape case, 25

Dahrendorf, Professor Ralf (Warden of St Anthony's College), on sexual harassment at Oxford University, 59
Daily Express: highlights dangers on public transport at night, 66–7; on the Kate Parkin case, 67; on the Linda Tolbert case, 163–4
Daily Mail: report on Liverpool City Council employee's sexual harassment of female colleague, 19; on sexual harassment of students at Oxford University, 59
Daily Mirror: interview with victim of husband's rape, 37; on Liz Berrisford case, 38; on Michael Alway case, 50–51; and the Tim Preston case,

107; Diana Lamplugh interview, 136
Daily Telegraph, 8; report on secretaries who suffer office stress, 39; reports Lynne Gunning case, 82, 83–4, 85–6
damages awarded for sexual harassment/sexual discrimination, 40, 55, 82, 85–6, 93, 113, 121, 153–4, 162–3
Daoud, Alex (Miami Beach mayor), and the Sunday Sanchez case, 91
Davaney, Liz (gym mistress), case of, 60
Davids, Carl (rapist), 24
dealing with sexual harassment, 46, 47, 56, 116–34, 151, 168
Dealing With Sexual Harassment (NALGO), 123–5
Dean, Brenda (General Secretary of SOGAT), on her experience of sexual harassment, 41–3; calls for protection against harassment on public transport, 66
Deleo, Rocco (Lieutenant, Miami Beach Police), 92
Dignity of Woman at Work (Michael Rubenstein), 127–34
Dirty Joke Brigade, 73–4
Dismore, Andrew (solicitor), on the Lynne Gunning case, 82, 162–3; on proliferation of sexual harassment cases, 166
dogs, men compared to, in their sexual behaviour, 96
dress, *see* provocative dress
driving instructors, sexual harassment by, 101–2

Edmonds, John (of GMB), on dealing with sexual harassment, 116
education, suggestion that subject of sexual harassment be part of school curriculum, 47
Edwards, Janet (of Crest Hotels), on adult films shown in hotels, 32–3
EEC, Michael Rubenstein's report for, 127–34
effects on women of sexual harassment, 15, 17, 52–5, 56, 58, 88–91
Elmslie, Lord, and the Jean Porcelli case, 152
EMAP publishing company and the Sally Muehring case, 154
employers, responsibilities under the Sex Discrimination Act, 46, 150–51
Employment Protection (Consolidation) Act 1978, 127
Equal Opportunities Commission, 28, 51, 54, 82, 170
Equal Pay Act, 14
exploitation of women as sex objects, 70–72

factories, women in, 140
female form, fascination of the, 70–72
Fenner, Dame Peggy, MP, 26
films: voyeurism in, 23–4; adult movies in hotels, 32–3
Fire Brigades' Union and the Soho Fire Station case, 85, 86, 87
Fire Service Disciplinary Code and the Lynne Gunning case, 82–3
Firefighter journal, 86
flashers, 141–2
Fletcher, Jenni (Labour councillor), and the Soho Fire Station case, 84–5
Foster, Jodie (actress), role in *The Accused*, 23, 26
Fox, Fiona (of EOC), 51

Fraser, Ian (barman), dismissed from post for verbal familiarity, 12

Freeman, Vaughan (motoring correspondent of *Today* newspaper), on sexual harassment by driving instructors, 102

Garbutt, Christine (of the *Daily Mirror*), on identifying sexual harassment, 46–8, 72, 92, 126

'girlie' magazines and calendars, 24, 99

Glassman, Kenneth (Miami Beach Police Chief), 91–2

GMB, positive action, 115–16, 117

Goodfellow, Len (fireman at Soho Fire Station), 78–9, 82, 83, 86

graffiti, 141

Grandison, Glen (fireman at Soho Fire Station), 82, 83

Greater London Council: compensation paid in Lynne Gunning case, 82, 85–6; Public Services and Fire Brigades Committee, 83, 84, 85

Green, Sir Allan QC, 34

Grieve, Lord, and the Jean Porcelli case, 152

Grigg, Alan (school headmaster), and the Liz Berrisford case, 38

Guardian, the: profile of Maurice Jones and the *Yorkshire Miner*, 65; picture of women firefighters, 77; on Soho Fire Station case, 85; quotes Karen Harrison, 158

Gunning, Lynne, case of, 77–87, 161–3, 168; experience in the London Fire Brigade, 77–87; experiences harassment after making formal complaint, 80–81; psychological effects of her experience, 81; employers proved to be in breach of common law, 161; settles out of court, 161–2

Hague, Helen (of the *Independent*), reports Karen Harrison's speech at TUC women's conference, 157–8

Haldane Society, 36

Hale, Sir Matthew (17th-century judge), disputes rape within marriage, 34

Hall, Anthea (of the *Sunday Telegraph*), on appearance as a professional requirement in any job, 137

Hall, Margaret (of *Today* newspaper), article on the Sunday Sanchez case, 88–92

Hampson, Gillian, sexual harassment victim, 121

'happily married men' as office sex pests, 40

Harman, Harriet, MP, on the law regarding sexual harassment, 85

Harper, Madeleine (of the *Mail on Sunday*), article on the Linda Tolbert case, 164–6

Harrison, Karen (British Rail train-driver), case of, 155–9, 168

Hebdomadal Council, Oxford University, and complaints by students of sexual harassment, 57, 59

Hempel, Sandra (of the *Sunday Times*), article on the Women's Legal Defence Fund, 169

Hemsley, Leslie (fireman at Soho Fire Station), 82, 83

Holiday Inn hotels, adult films shown in, 33

Hollingsworth, Liz (woman firefighter), 77

180

Home Office, advice list to men in helping to remove fears of women, 148–9
homes, safety in, after dark, 66
Hope, Brian (rapist), 24–5
hotels: businesswomen staying in, 32–3; porno films in, 32–3; female staff as victims, 95–6
Howarth, Barry (of NALGO), on the Tim Preston case, 106, 107, 110, 111
Humphries, Barry, humour of, 76
Hyatt v. *Smithko*, 127

identification of sexual harassment, 11–16
Incomes Data Services and the Jean Porcelli case, 153
Independent, the: reports bogus-taxi incident, 145–6; reports Karen Harrison's speech at TUC women's conference, 157
induction ceremonies of London Fire Brigade, 82–3
industrial relations, women in a man's world, 77–93, 155–9
Irving, Barry (of the Police Foundation), on research into minicab attacks, 147

Joeman, L.M., *The Risks in Going to Work*, 142–5
Johnstone, Violet (of the *Sunday Telegraph*), interviews Diana Lamplugh, 136
Jones, Maurice (editor), on pin-ups in the *Yorkshire Miner*
judges, tolerant views of male assaults on women, 67–8

Kall-Kwick Printing, survey on secretaries and office stress, 39
Kane, Peter (of the *Daily Mirror*), covers the Dawn Blighton case, 18
Keane, Sue (consumer psychologist), on secretaries and office stress, 39
Kennedy, Joe (Commander), and the Soho Fire Station case, 87
Kerrigan, Justine (actress), on her role as sexual harassment victim in *Brookside*, 43–4
Kiley, Sam (higher education reporter), on sexual harassment of university students, 57, 58
Kingsmill, Denise, on sexual harassment of women in working life, 56; and the Sally Muehring case, 154; on proliferation of sexual harassment cases, 166
Kitson, Carolyn, 'sex-pest' victim, 39–40
Knight, Dame Jill, MP, 24, 25
Kojak (TV series), 24
Kusbit, Sandra (woman police officer), and the Sunday Sanchez case, 92

Labour Research Department 'Bargaining Report' article, 122–3
Lamplugh, Diana, work of, 135–49
Lamplugh, Suzy, disappearance of, 135–7; *see also* Suzy Lamplugh Trust
Lane, Lord Chief Justice, on rape within marriage, 33–4
Langford, Garry (fireman involved in Soho Fire Station case), 78–80, 82, 84, 85, 86
Law concerning rape within marriage, 33–7, 167–8
Lawson, Sir Frederick, on rape within marriage, 34–5
Lawton, Lord Justice, 127

legal aid for sexual harassment cases, 151, 169–71
Lightfoot, Liz (Education Correspondent of the *Mail on Sunday*), on sexual harassment of students at Oxford University, 59
Listener, The, review of *The Accused* (film), 23; on rape within marriage, 34; on comedian Max Miller, 75
Liverpool City Council and the Vince Birkhead case, 19–21
Livingstone, Ken, and the Soho Fire Station case, 85
London Borough Grants Scheme aids Women's Legal Defence Fund, 169
London Fire Brigade, and the Lynne Gunning case, 77–87
Lord, Steven (rapist), 29
Losinka, Mrs Kate, and incident at CPSA conference, 7–8
Loveless, Elisa, victim in the Michael Alway case, 49–50, 52, 54
Lowry, Judge Nina, and the Dawn Blighton case, 18; and South London rape case, 25
Luciznksas, Anthony (sex pest), 18
lust v. love, 71–2

McDonough, Mike (journalist), on the Blondina Ortega case, 29
McGahey, Mick, 12
McNeill, Isola (of the *Morning Star*), on the Karen Harrison case, 156–7
magazines, pornographic, 24–6
Mahon, Alice, MP: on safety in minicabs, 146; welcomes advice code to men, 149
Mail on Sunday: on the Blondina Ortega case, 29; on sexual harassment of students at Oxford University, 59; on minicab attacks, 146; on the Linda Tolbert case, 164–6
Mainstone, Valerie: views on women's dress, 27–8; on the work of WASH, 44–5, 46; on dealing with sexual harassment, 104
male attitudes to women, 58, 69–76
man's world, women in a, 77–93, 155–9
marriage, rape within, 33–7
Martin, Angela (sex therapist), on porn films in hotels, 32
Meade-King, Maggy (of the *Guardian*), quotes Karen Harrison, 158
Medawar, Judge Nicholas, tolerant view of sex harassment case, 67–8
members of Parliament demand action against pornography, 24
men, advice code, 149, 160–61
Miami Beach, case of Police Patrolwoman Sunday Sanchez, 88–93
'mild' sexual harassment, 11–12, 47
Miller, Max (comedian), ban by BBC, 74–6
Milmo, Mr John, QC, 34
Mills, Billy (of NUPE), on the Vince Birkhead case, 19
Minicab Association, 146
minicabs, dangers of travelling by, 145–8
Missing Persons Bureau, Diana Lamplugh lays foundation for, 136
Monteith, Maggie, founds the Women's Legal Defence Fund, 169, 170–71
Moore, Suzanne (journalist), reviews *The Accused* (film), 23
Morning Star, on the Karen Harrison case, 156–7, 158

motivation for sexual harassment, 11
Ms London (giveaway magazine), report on telephone pests, 102–3
Muehring, Sally: case of, 153–5; on sex harassment as power-play, 166–7

NALGO, 17, 19, 20; and the Tim Preston case, 106; *Dealing with Sexual Harassment* pamphlet, 123–5; positive action of, 121, 123–5
Neves, Viv (model), 70
New Internationalist, 'dos and don'ts' charter aimed at men, 160–61
New Statesman, review of *The Accused* (film), 23
News of the World, reporter at CPSA conference, Brighton, 7–8
Nichols, Peter (writer): on Barry Humphries' humour, 76; on Max Miller's humour, 75
non-admission by men of sexual harassment, 46
North Lonsdale Hospital, Medical Records Officer sexual harassment case, 8–9, 105–14
Nuffield Foundation aids Women's Legal Defence Fund, 169
'numbers game' played by some men, 71
NUPE, 19; positive action by, 119–21
NUT: guidelines on sexual harassment, 60–63; positive action, 121

obscene telephone calls, 102–3
ogling, 19, 20, 99
O'Mara, Maureen (NUPE Women's Officer), on dealing with sexual harassment, 119–21
Ortega, Blondina, case of, 29–31
Oulton, Charles, on sexual harassment of students at Oxford University, 58–9
Ousedale School, Newport Pagnell, case of Liz Davaney, 60
Owen, Mr Justice, on rape within marriage, 34
Owens, Bernard (tribunal chairman in the Owen Brown case), 40
Oxford University: code of conduct and disciplinary framework set up to deal with sexual harassment complaints, 57; harassment of students by dons, 58–9

page-3 pin-ups, 25, 45
Painter, Kate (crime expert), on rape within marriage, 36
Parkin, Kate (of the *Daily Express*): interviews sexual harassment victim, 67; on the Linda Tolbert case, 163–4
Parkinson, Cecil, campaign against sexual harassment on public transport, 66–7
Patten, John, launches advice list to men on behaviour towards women, 149
Pattinson, Terry, interviews Diana Lamplugh, 136–7
Peen, John (station officer), and the Soho Fire Station case, 79, 82, 83–4, 86–7
Phillips, Dr Celia, *The Risks in Going to Work*, 142–5
photographic models, 70–71
pin-ups, 25, 45
Police Foundation, support for research into minicab attacks, 146–7
Porcelli, Mrs Jean, case of, 38, 151–3

pornography, 24–6, 32–3, 70–71
Portillo, Michael, and aid to Suzy Lamplugh Trust, 146
power over women, men's use of, 41–68, 103–4; *see also* man's world, women in a
Practical Ways to Crack Crime (Home Office), 148–9
Preston, Tim, case of, 8–9, 105–14, 168
Priestley, Richard (of South Cumbria Health Authority), and the Tim Preston case, 9, 107, 113
Proops, Marje, on women's dress, 1–2, 22, 26–7
Prosser, Margaret (of the TGWU), on dealing with sexual harassment, 125–7
provocative female dress, 21–2, 23, 24, 26–9
psychological effects on victims, 15, 17, 52–5, 56, 58, 88–91
public transport: campaign against sexual harassment on, 66–7; minicab attacks, 145–8

Quinn, John (of the *Mail on Sunday*), report on minicab attacks, 146

rape: films and magazines, link with, 23–6; within marriage, 33–7; attacks on women in their homes after dark, 66
Reed Employment, funds *The Risks in Going to Work* report, 142
Reid, George, involvement in the Jean Porcelli case, 152–3
Richardson, Jo, MP, 167
Richardson, Wayne (molester), 67, 68
Riddell, Mary (of the *Daily Mirror*), on the Michael Alway case, 50–51; on women's dress, 28
Rieden, Juliet (reporter), on telephone sex pests, 102
Risks in Going to Work, The (Phillips, Stockdale and Joeman), 142–5
Robinson, Anne (of the *Daily Mirror*), on sexual harassment, 19–21
Ross, Sarah (student), on sexual harassment of students at Oxford University, 59
Rubenstein, Michael (Industrial Law Society chairman), report for European Commission, 127–34
Ruddock, Joan, MP, 24
Russell, Peter (General Secretary, Driving Instructors' Association), on sexual harassment by driving instructors, 102

St Mary and St Anne School, Abbots Bromley, sex discrimination case, 38
Sampson, Val (journalist), interview with Justine Kerrigan, 43–4
Sanchez, Sunday (Miami Beach patrolwoman), case of, 88–93
Sanchez, Tony (husband of Sunday), 93
Scarborough, Bonnie (Women's Officer, St Edmund's College), on academics' attitude to women in the classroom, 58
Scargill, Arthur, and pin-ups in the *Yorkshire Miner*, 64–5
schools, sexual harassment of staff and pupils, 60–64
Scotland: rape within marriage, 35; case of Mrs J. Porcelli, 38, 151–3
secretaries, office stress experienced by, 39–40, 95–6
self-help against sexual harassment, 26

Sex Discrimination Act 1975, 14, 127, 150, 151
Sex in the Office, Alfred Marks Bureau survey, 97–101
sex-stereotyping, 160
Sexual Harassment at Work, TUC booklet, 12–16
Short, Clare, MP, 25–6
Short, Stephen (sub officer at Soho Fire Station), 82, 83
Simpson, Stewart, prosecutor in the Linda Tolbert case, 164
Society of Civil and Public Servants, positive action, 121
Soho Fire Station, the Lynne Gunning case, 77–87, 161–3, 168
South Cumbria Health Authority, employers of Tim Preston, 107, 112
Steedman, Claire (of Cambridge University Students' Union), on survey of sexual harassment of students, 57
Stinson, Marnie, victim in the Michael Alway case, 49–50, 52–5
Stockdale, Dr Jan, *The Risks in Going to Work*, 142–5
Stone, Chris (sexual harasser), 60
Strathclyde Regional Council, and the case of Mrs Porcelli, 151–3
streakers, 141
Sun newspaper, and the Michael Alway case, 49, 55–6; on rape within marriage, 36
Sunday Telegraph: on sexual harassment of university students, 58–9; Diana Lamplugh interview, 136; article on professional requirements for appearance in any job, 137
Sunday Times, article on Women's Legal Defence Fund, 169
surveys, 34, 39, 57–8, 97–101

Suzy Lamplugh Trust, 135–6; *The Risks in Going to Work* report, 142–5; *Tips to Promote Safer Mini-Cabbing*, 146–8

Teachers, NUT's guidelines to, 60–63
telephone sex pests, 102–3
television programmes, link with rape offences, 24
terms used by older married men in reference to their spouses, 74
TGWU: positive action, 121, 125–7; *Combating Sexual Harassment* booklet, 125
Thompson, Caro (journalist), interviews Marnie Stinson, 52
Times, The: survey at Cambridge University among female undergraduates, 57; adverts featuring Viv Neves, 70; report of the Sally Muehring case, 153–4, 155
Tips to Promote Safer Mini-Cabbing (Suzy Lamplugh Trust), 146–8
Titre, Gifford (rapist), 24
Today newspaper: on adult films in hotels, 32; on rape within marriage, 36; on sex pests, 60; on Kate Parkin case, 67–8; on Lynne Gunning case, 78–9, 80, 82; on the Sunday Sanchez case, 88–92; on sexual harassment by driving instructors, 102; interviews Ann Widdecombe MP, 149
Tolbert, Linda, case of, 163–6
'touchers', 72, 98–9
Toyne, Patrick (fireman), involvement in the Soho Fire Station case, 78, 79, 82, 83, 86
trade unions, 12–16, 17, 19, 20–21, 28, 60–65, 106–7, 115–25, 162

Trades Union Congress: guidelines regarding sexual harassment, 12–16; attitude to the problem, 115; Karen Harrison's motion at women's conference, 155–6

traffic wardens, female, as victims, 95

transport, campaign against sexual harassment on public, 66–7; *see also* minicabs

Trusthouse Forte, no adult films screened in hotels of, 33

TUC, 12–16, 115, 155–6

Turner, Jonathan (lawyer), on rape within marriage, 36–7

Turner, Mrs Pat (National Equal Rights Officer of GMB), on dealing with sexual harassment, 116–19

types of men who become sex pests, 73, 139–40

typical behaviour of the sex pest, 51, 94–5

United States: case of Blondina Ortega, 29–31; case of Sunday Sanchez, 88–93; Equal Opportunities Commission, 92–3

university students, sexual harassment of, 57–60

USDAW, positive action, 121–2

Violence Against Women (Elizabeth Wilson), 104

Wade, Dorothy (of *The Sunday Times*), on Michael Alway case, 55–6

Waksler, Bernard (US civil rights lawyer), 93

Walsh, Jan (of British Telecom), on telephone sex pests, 103

Walters, Margaret (of *The Listener*), reviews *The Accused* (film), 23

Walton, Brian (industrial tribunal chairman in the Michael Alway case), 49

Walton, Sir John (of Oxford University), on sexual harassment of university students and staff, 59

WASH, 27, 44–6, 104, 138, 151

Western Excavating v. *Sharp*, 127

Whitburn, Vanessa (*Brookside* producer), on portrayal of victim in TV series, 44

Widdecombe, Ann, MP, 149

Wilenius, Paul (political editor of *Today* newspaper), on rape within marriage, 36

Williams, Leon (molester), 67

Wilson, Elizabeth, *Violence Against Women*, 104

Wilson, Glenn (psychologist), on the serious sex pest, 60

women: reluctance to report sexual harassment, 16–17; provocative dress, 21–2, 23, 24, 26–9; in subordinate roles, 46; dealing with sexual harassment, 46, 47, 56, 116–34, 151, 168; exploitation as sex objects, 70–72; in a man's world, 77–93, 155–9

Women Against Sexual Harassment (WASH), 27, 44–6, 104, 138, 151

Women's Legal Defence Fund, 151, 169–71

World in Action, survey on rape within marriage, 34, 36

Yorkshire Miner, pin-ups in, 64–5

Young, Andrew (of *Today* newspaper), on businesswomen, treatment in hotels of, 32

YTS students, victims in the Tim Preston case, 106, 110, 114

Yusuf, Mohammed (sex pest), 164–6